SELECTING LIBRARY FURNITURE:

A Guide for Librarians, Designers, and Architects

by Carol R. Brown

ORYX PRESS
1989

The rare Arabian Oryx is believed to have inspired the myth of the unicorn. This desert antelope became virtually extinct in the early 1960s. At that time several groups of international conservationists arranged to have 9 animals sent to the Phoenix Zoo to be the nucleus of a captive breeding herd. Today the Oryx population is nearly 800, and over 400 have been returned to reserves in the Middle East.

Cover Photograph courtesy of Vecta®

Copyright © 1989 by Carol R. Brown
Published by The Oryx Press
2214 North Central at Encanto
Phoenix, Arizona 85004-1483

Published simultaneously in Canada

Printed and Bound in the United States of America

∞ The paper used in this publication meets the minimum requirements of American National Standard for Information Science—Permanence of Paper for Printed Library Materials, ANSI Z39.48, 1984.

Library of Congress Cataloging-in-Publication Data

Brown, Carol R.
   Selecting library furniture : a guide for librarians, designers, and architects / by Carol R. Brown.
      p.   cm.
   Bibliography: p.
   Includes index.
   ISBN 0-89774-535-3
   1. Library fittings and supplies—Purchasing. 2. Library architecture. 3. Library buildings. I. Title.
Z684.B86   1989
022'.9—dc20   89-9224

In Memory of
Ann Rowland Flores
1936–1987

Contents

Acknowledgments

Over the past three years, I have discussed furnishings with many of my colleagues and with countless people working in the furniture and shelving industries. I appreciate all of the information I have gathered from these conversations.

I would particularly like to thank Robert Boardman for the information he supplied, for his patience in answering my questions, and for his understanding of my desire to raise the level of quality in the library furniture industry. I am also grateful to Bruce Pike and Tom Maloy, who were especially supportive of this project and gladly shared their knowledge and expertise with me. In addition, I would like to thank the following people for their assistance: Tom Dietrich, Pierre Husson, Connie Pine, Bruce Simoneaux, and Frank Yench. I also wish to extend thanks to Carl Eckelman for his work in the area of performance testing, on which I relied when writing the chapters on tables and chairs. The following companies should be acknowledged for their assistance: Brodart, Buckstaff, Estey, Library Bureau, Meridian, Modulex, Texwood, Steelcase, and Worden. Thanks are also given to David Henington for his continuing support both while I was at Houston Public Library and since I left that organization.

On a personal note, I wish to acknowledge my photographer, David Lund, and his assistant, Laurel Lund, and my artist, Martha Andress. Special words of gratitude go to Joyce Claypool, my literary agent, editor, adviser, publicist, and trainer. Thank you, Joyce, especially for helping me to pack a tighter suitcase and showing me what true friendship really is. I would be remiss if I did not mention the two most important people in my life: my sons, Ian and Kevin Brown. Thank you both for providing unquestioning support for me through all of my changes over the past three years. You are exemplary young adults. And, thank you, Eric, for letting me go gracefully.

Preface

From 1975 to 1988, while I was at Houston Public Library, I had an opportunity to work on many aspects of the building and refurbishing of library facilities; in the early 1980s, I began consulting in that area, also. While I was working on the Helen Hall Library in League City, Texas, I researched construction of the furnishings to be selected and designed custom features for many of the pieces. I worked with the architect, Blair Hamilton, and the librarian, Susan Mathews, in developing a color scheme for the building and choosing fabrics and finishes. This experience demonstrated that my earlier training in the fine arts was particularly applicable in planning library interiors. Over the next year, I became increasingly interested in the construction of furnishings and the elements that determine high quality in a piece of furniture.

Most of my consulting jobs took me to small municipal libraries in Texas, and I soon realized that librarians in these small towns often relied entirely on others—salespeople, architects, designers—in planning the library interior. In time, it became apparent to me that librarians in all kinds and sizes of facilities had little information available to guide them in the process of selecting furnishings.

In 1986 and 1987, I had an opportunity to attend the Management Development Program at Texas A & M University and a seminar on marketing at Southern Methodist University; soon after, I was asked to prepare a marketing plan for Houston Public Library. At that time, I planned to combine two of my special interests and write a magazine article about the part that interior design plays in marketing library services. As I investigated related sources, I found that there were numerous articles and books about various subjects related to the planning of library interiors. It had been several years, however, since a book on library furniture had been published, and I realized that a book, rather than an article, was needed to provide the kind of comprehensive information that would be useful today for librarians facing the prospect of selecting furnishings for their facility.

Since related topics, such as space planning and the use of color, are covered in other books, I decided to limit my discussion to the furnishings themselves. The items covered are freestanding pieces that are not necessarily part of the basic structure of the building. I have not discussed, for example, carpet or other floor coverings, millwork that is part of a building contract, light fixtures, etc.

Some of what is here can be found in other sources. I hope, however, that I have provided a service by gathering and organizing this information, and by adding my own observations and experience concerning the construction of furnishings. My goal was to provide a tool that can be used to guide decision makers through the furniture selection process. I have tried, as much as possible, to provide criteria for selection without overwhelming the reader with my personal preferences. I believe that each individual should use the information I have given here to make an independent decision as to what is best for her/his library or office. I am a librarian by profession, and this book is written primarily to assist librarians. I am hopeful, however, that others involved in the selection process and those in the library furniture industry will find the information useful.

Chapter 1
Introduction to the Selection Process

For many librarians, the selection of furniture for a new building or the major refurbishing of an existing facility is a once-in-a-lifetime task. The project usually involves a number of people in addition to the librarian: architects, facilities planners, interior designers, purchasing agents, library board members, friends of the library, and members of governing bodies. Many of these individuals will view themselves as the real professionals and decision makers in the project. The library manager, the staff members, and the users are, however, the ones who will remain on the site, long after the others are gone, to test whether the design of the building and the furnishings selected are satisfactory.

In large projects with generous funding, an interior designer or consultant is hired to do the space planning and select the furnishings. Sometimes this person is a member of the architectural firm. In other situations, facilities planners and purchasing agents may be more involved in the selection. For many libraries, small as well as large, the selection of furnishings is the responsibility of someone with little or no background for the task. In that case, however, there are any number of salespeople who will be glad to step in and take over a project. Some salespeople will assure the less-than-confident librarian that her/his product is the very best for the price, will talk enough technical language to reassure the librarian that s/he is an authority on the subject of library furnishings, and will offer to do the complete project: write specifications, lay out the area, select finishes, etc.

The result may or may not be satisfactory. The librarian may end up with furniture or shelving that does not accomplish the intended purpose, will not withstand heavy, long-term use, and is not particularly attractive. In any case, the fact remains that the librarian did not go through a process of determining how to obtain the very best furnishings for the available money. The library is not just a general office area; its space has a very specific function that must be addressed in furnishing the interior. The person who knows the most about the needs of the library is the manager. The librarian *is* the professional in this situation, and has the responsibility to make the right recommendations with regard to the furnishings and to have the confidence to ask reasonable questions of the design professionals and vendors involved in the project.

The information included here is written to provide such librarians with the foundation they need to make furniture selections themselves, or to work confidently and knowledgeably with design professionals. The librarian should not assume that an interior designer, architect, or consultant necessarily knows what is best for any particular facility. Many design professionals may be award-winners when it comes to selecting furnishings for general office space, but they may never have been involved in a library project. They may be more interested in making the area aesthetically pleasing according to current trends in interior design than in designing a usable facility.

Furnishings for offices are often selected to be used only by the staff for five to ten years before being replaced. Library furnishings, however, are selected to be used by the public or a group of users, in addition to the staff. In many instances, the larger items are expected to be serviceable for the lifetime of the library—30, 40, even 50 years. Even designers who *have* worked on library projects will not be as attuned to the needs of the staff and users as the library manager is. This is not to say that the professional hired to select the furniture on the project will not do a good job. The best assurance, however, for obtaining a functional and attractive library interior is for a librarian to be actively involved in the project. S/he should feel free to ask questions and offer suggestions until s/he is satisfied that the furnishings selected are satisfactory.

In the past, libraries were seen as specialized institutions with stereotypical needs in furnishings. Most library chairs and tables looked about the same—sturdy and nondescript. Library interiors were generally pleasant but serviceable, institutional-looking places without much distinction. Now that librarians are interested in marketing their services and merchandising their products, however, plan-

Figure 1. When Houston Public Library's Young Branch opened in 1957, it was furnished with standard wooden tables, chairs, and shelving manufactured by a library furniture manufacturer. *Photograph courtesy of Houston Public Library.*

Figure 2. Stanaker Branch, Houston Public Library, opened in 1985, with steel shelving, paperback racks, and chairs and tables made by contract office furniture manufacturers. *Photo: Lacey Flagg.*

ning the library interior is not such a limited task. Unfortunately, many librarians continue to approach such planning as they did in the past. They begin the process of furniture selection by looking at what is available. This leaves the responsibility for the end result with the manufacturers. It would be better if librarians generally took responsibility for informing the manufacturers of what is needed in the library.

In order to do this, the furniture selection process should include more than just considering what is available. Rather, the process should include the following steps in order: (1) determine what the furnishings should accomplish for the particular library involved; (2) consider what is available on the market, or what can be obtained to fulfill the requirements determined in step 1; and, (3) make the selections and purchases.

The following chapters should provide useful information for architects, designers, or vendors who will be involved in library building/remodeling projects for the first time. Librarians who expect to work closely with citizens' groups or library boards can pass this information on to those groups in order to improve communications concerning the selections made for the facility and the expenditure of funds. Furniture manufacturers and salespeople may want to read this book in order to improve their knowledge of the market from the viewpoint of the librarian.

Chapter 2 discusses the process for determining furniture requirements and provides examples of applying the process to particular items. Chapters 3 through 9 provide background information about construction and discuss particular kinds of furnishings and shelving available. The last two chapters discuss bid procedures and the library market.

Although the products of specific manufacturers are discussed, the reader should note that these items are used only as examples. The emphasis is on the criteria for evaluating products—those now available and those to be manufactured in the future. Specific products are discussed to answer questions concerning what particular qualities and materials make some of them more reliable, more serviceable, etc., than others. The resulting criteria or considerations for evaluating a product can then also be applied to brands not mentioned here, or not yet manufactured. The reader is cautioned not to assume that because a product is *not* discussed here, it is not therefore worthy of consideration, nor that inclusion of a particular brand constitutes an endorsement of that product.

Chapter 2
Determining What Is Needed

The first step in planning a new library is the preparation of a building program, which serves as a guide to the architect or other professionals designing the facility. The program defines the environment in which the facility will be built, outlines the general requirements of the building from the standpoint of the owner, and describes the functions and relative size of various spaces. The architect interprets the program guidelines set down by the owner, and translates the information into a set of drawings that can be used to construct the building.

Similarly, the process of selecting library furnishings should begin with the development of a set of guidelines to be used in determining the specific products to be purchased. This "furniture program" may be a written document or just informal notes. In either case, the information will be used by the librarian when making specific furniture selections her/himself, or in guiding others involved in decision making: by the interior designer or consultant hired to write specifications; by the architectural firm assisting with the selection of furnishings; or by a purchasing agent responsible for the acquisition of the interior items.

Whether a project involves furnishing a public, school, academic, or special library, the initial task in the selection process is to establish just what the owner of the facility wants or needs to accomplish with the various items purchased. As a rule, this will depend on many of the general functions and requirements as spelled out in the building program; for example, the primary building use; the age of the users; the amount of use expected; the kinds of materials to be stored, organized, and displayed; the number of staff members; future changes anticipated; etc. More specifically, three major factors should be considered when making furniture selections: the function of the item, its maintenance, and its appearance.

The function consideration will include determining not only *what* use will be made of the item, but *who* will use it and *how* it will be used. In some cases, function may further involve deciding how long the item will be used at any one time, how often it will be used, and whether the uses may change in the future. Maintenance considerations include the ability to withstand heavy use over a long period of time, ease of day-to-day cleaning and upkeep, ease with which repairs can be made or parts replaced, and flexibility of the item in regard to changing its location or use in the future. Evaluating the appearance of the item will, of course, involve considering how it adds to the attractiveness of the building, whether it is compatible with the other furnishings and the design of the building, and whether it contributes to the general atmosphere desired for the facility.

Other examples of function, maintenance, and appearance will be given later, as the process is applied in individual situations. While each of the three factors should be considered, those bearing the most weight in making any given selection will, of course, depend on the particular circumstances. For example, in selecting task chairs, function and maintenance may be more important than appearance. When choosing chairs for the board room, on the other hand, appearance may be a more important factor than maintenance.

While the librarian or other professional in charge of the process has responsibility for the final selections, as in other managerial decision making, input from library staff is essential. The staff needs to provide specific information about what kind of furnishings they think will improve their working environment and help them to increase productivity. Ideally, some input from library users or potential users should also be obtained.

Very useful information can be obtained from the staff of a recently constructed facility that has been used for at least a year. The project can be discussed with the manager by phone, or better yet, a visit can be made to the facility. The staff can be questioned as to what does or doesn't function well and what the users like or don't like. When visiting the site, it is possible to see which furnishings still look new after some public use and which ones show signs of wear. It is helpful to talk to the staff member in charge of maintaining the building in order to find out which furnishings are easy to clean and which ones are difficult to maintain. It is also useful to sit down in the chairs to see if they are comfortable, look at how well the circulation desk functions for the staff, shake the shelves to check their stability, and notice which furniture is getting the most use by patrons.

On the basis of input from the staff, the building program, and other information gathered, the qualities desired in the various items to be purchased can be determined. These ideas, regardless of whether they become a formal document or remain as notes for future reference, become the furniture program. The furniture and shelving layout and the quantities of items to be purchased vary in academic, public, special, and school libraries. The furniture and shelving used are the same, however, regardless of the kind of library: reading tables and chairs, bookstacks, index tables, or carrels.

The following examples are notes written for reading chairs for a fictitious public library, but the same kind of notes can describe any furnishings to be used in any kind of library situation. In deciding which reading chair to purchase, the staff might outline their ideas in the following manner:

Reading chair for adults:

Function. For the new library, we want a chair that is comfortable for reading or study for long periods of time (as long as two or three hours). We want a chair that has plenty of padding on the seat and back, so we want one that has a wooden frame and an upholstered seat and back. The chair should have good back support and a seat large enough to be comfortable for both large- and average-sized users. We have decided that a chair with arms is desirable for our users. Since we will have carpet, the chair must be designed with a sled base so that it can easily be pulled up to or away from the table.

(Or the choice might be a chair with a metal frame with a chrome or epoxy finish, or an all-wood chair, or one with vinyl upholstery. The library may opt for a chair with no arms, and a leg rather than sled base.)

Maintenance. The reading chair should be one that has been performance-tested and has proven to be sturdy enough to withstand heavy use for at least 15 years. The legs should not break if someone rocks back and forth in the chair. The arms should be at the correct height to fit under the edge of the table without doing damage to either the arms or the table edge. The chair should have fabric that can be easily maintained and cleaned and should have a design that makes it easy to reupholster. The chair should not have a crevice between the seat and back where dirt can collect. The chair should be constructed so that it will not come apart where the various parts are joined. The back of the chair should be attached to the seat in such a manner that the back will not break away from the seat.

(Maintenance considerations might include choosing specific materials because of ease of upkeep; e.g., vinyl rather than fabric upholstery.)

Appearance. Since the building is fairly traditional, we want a reading chair that is attractive but compatible with the design of the library, including the wooden staircase. If possible, we want a chair with a slight arch across the back, or some other element to give it a little distinction. Since the library board has indicated a strong interest in a dark oak finish on the staircase, we want to choose a wooden frame that will blend well with the wood used in the building itself.

Other seating for adults in the public area could include stools or benches for use at index tables or tables holding various kinds of equipment such as CD-ROMs or terminals. In this case, considering the function of the item, seating without a back may be desired in order to discourage users from tying up the equipment by using the seat for reading or studying. Here again, other options to be considered might be a sled or leg base and upholstered, wood, or metal seat. With stools, maintenance and appearance considerations may be similar to those for the chairs. On the other hand, if there are other kinds of materials in the building or other design elements that are significant, the appearance of the stool could be tied in more with those other elements rather than with the chairs.

In a children's area, the function consideration of chairs should include the fact that the chairs will inevitably be used for activities other than sitting, including climbing, jumping, piling, and building. Also, chairs of more than one height should be provided to accommodate children of different ages. Even the smallest chairs will also be used by parents, and should be strong enough to hold adults. In the children's area, maintenance is a very important consideration for any seating provided. Just as it does for adults, the library may wish to use several kinds of seating—chairs at reading tables, stools at tables where audio-visual equipment is used, step stools scattered around the picture book area, or cushions.

While the function of a lounge chair is easily distinguished from the use of a reading chair at a table in the library environment, the library function of a lounge chair differs clearly from the corresponding use of this type of furniture in other waiting areas, such as in the airport or a doctor's reception room. In the airport, for example, rows of ganged (connected) seats are used by waiting passengers who are willing to sit elbow-to-elbow for short periods of time out of necessity. As research on personal space has indicated, however, many of us are uncomfortable sitting this close to a stranger. Users in library situations, then, with a choice of seats, will not take the chair that puts them right next to another person. Lounge furniture in the library may be used for long periods of time by someone reading, or for a short time by someone taking a break from studying. In either case, long sofas, or the type of ganged seating used in waiting areas, will not be particularly functional because of people's feelings about personal space.

Maintenance considerations for lounge furniture will certainly be important in public areas with heavy use. The amount and kind of upholstery, the choice of material used for the frame, and the design of the chair will all affect maintenance. For example, the library may want a chair upholstered with fabric because it is comfortable and attractive. On the other hand, the choice may be one that has an upholstered seat and back, but with wooden or metal arms, because they are the parts of the lounge chair that get dirty most quickly with heavy use.

Lounge furniture is used not only to provide an alternate form of seating, but also to break up the monotony of having rows and rows of reading tables or ranges of shelving. In other words, such furniture plays a definite role in the appearance of the library. Large, comfortable-looking chairs make the interior more inviting, and suggest that the library is a pleasant place to spend some time, perhaps doing some leisure reading. The style of chair used can also be significant in relating the furnishings to the design of the building, and in contributing to the particular atmosphere desired. For example, a large, fully upholstered lounge chair may be appropriate in some libraries, while a sled-base chair with an epoxy-coated metal frame and an upholstered seat and back may be a better choice in another building.

Function will be the highest priority to consider when choosing chairs to be used by the staff. Several different kinds of chairs may eventually be selected because of the variety of tasks carried out by the staff. Some staff members will need to have a chair that allows them to work comfortably when seated in front of a terminal or typewriter for long periods of time. The reference staff will probably need chairs that will allow them to sit comfortably but get up and down easily and frequently. Because many chairs in the library have to be shared by several staff members, ease of adjustability for different-sized individuals is important. Some chairs will need to be the right height for a 29″ worksurface and some may be needed for worksurfaces 38″ to 42″ high.

A chair that can be cleaned easily is, of course, desirable. The kind of upholstery selected, the availability of replacement parts, and the ease with which the chair can be reupholstered or repaired are also important maintenance considerations.

The appearance of the work chair plays an interesting role in the library, as in other office settings, in identifying the chain of command. The higher in the hierarchy the staff member is, the larger and more expensive the chair will be. The clerk in the workroom at the terminal sits in a secretarial posture chair with no arms and a low, or intermediate, back height. Reference librarians are more likely to have a full back and arms on their chairs, while the manager will have an executive chair with a high back and fully upholstered arms. In many cases, the chairs may be equally functional for the situation in which they are used, but they do play a role in office politics: the boss wants a larger, more elaborate chair that represents her/his status in the chain of command. Other appearance considerations are the upholstery, style, and base finish.

In determining the library's needs in reading tables, functional considerations will be fairly simple. The table's height depends on its use and the age of its users: 29″ high for adults reading and studying; 27″ high for young adults; 26″ high for typing height; and 20″ to 25″ high for children. The size and shape of tables needed will depend on whether users will be working singly or in groups, how much material they will need to spread out on the table, and whether they will use equipment on the worksurface. Some tables may include electrical raceways and a wire management system or task lighting, depending on their function.

The description of reading tables could very simply be as follows:

Reading tables:

Function. We want reading tables for adults that are 29″ high, which can be used for reading and studying for long periods of time. Most of our users will work alone or with one or two other people, so we want several tables to seat no more than four people. We want some rectangular tables, 42″ × 66″, and some 48″ round tables. In the children's area, we want some tables small enough for preschoolers and some for children in K–3rd grades. We also want two or three tables 27″ high, if there is enough room. Four tables, 48″ × 72″, equipped with an electrical raceway and wire management system, will be needed for the catalog.

The construction and finish of the table top are major elements in maintenance considerations for tables. The library might choose a table top constructed of butcher block, three-ply flakeboard, or five-ply lumber core. In some situations, a veneer or other wood surface can be maintained on a day-to-day basis and, if necessary, refinished. In libraries that are used heavily by the public, a high-pressure laminate may be maintained more easily, and for a longer period of time. The strength of a table depends on the materials used in the base and the joinery between the base and top. Because these

Figure 3. Work chairs are often selected from a "family" of chairs, so that every staff member has a high-quality chair appropriate for the task to be performed. Shown here are Vecta's Wilkhahn FS chairs, designed by Klaus Franck and Werner Sauer. *Photograph courtesy of Vecta®.*

elements affect how sturdy the table will be, they are important maintenance considerations; tables will be discussed further in Chapter 7.

Appearance considerations for a table include the materials used, the design or style, and the finish. A leg, panel end, or pedestal table could be chosen, with either a wood or metal base, in any number of different styles and finishes.

Decisions regarding index and stand-up reference tables, staff work tables, folding tables for meeting rooms, carrels, and stations for microform readers will include considerations similar to those noted here for reading tables. In the same building, the staff might decide to have some leg tables for reading, and tables with panel ends for holding microform readers. They might want to have rectangular tables that have wooden legs, while they prefer a metal base for round tables. Because it is desirable to have the design of all of the furnishings coordinated, decisions regarding tables will probably determine the style of such technical pieces as the index tables and atlas and dictionary stands.

Circulation and reference desks are the major workstations for interacting with the library's public, so the staff should consider the function, maintenance, and appearance of these items very carefully and thoroughly. The description of the function of the circulation desk, for example, should include how many people will be working there, what they will be doing, how they will do it, and what equipment will be used.

Function. The circulation desk should be large enough to accommodate three people working there at any one time. We want one workstation at sit-down height (29″) and at least two stations at stand-up height (38″–39″). The workstations should be open under the desk for knee space. Because we don't know what kind of equipment we will be using in the future, we want the stations at stand-up height to have one continuous flat surface. We want the top to be 27″ to 32″ wide, so it will be wide enough for equipment, but not too wide to reach across to hand books to patrons. If possible, the desk top should be built in such a manner that electrical cords from equipment can go down through the top at 12″ intervals or less, so that equipment can be moved along the surface as library needs change. Under the desk, there should be a wire management system to handle the cords and cables from telephones, datalines, terminals, etc. We will need at least nine linear feet of shelf space to store books we are holding for users. We will need one locking drawer equipped to hold cash, and two or three other drawers to hold office supplies. One of these drawers should be deep enough to hold charging trays full of transaction cards. One section of the desk should hold a twelve-drawer card catalog for patron records, fines, etc.

The staff might also want other kinds of units in the circulation desk, such as vertical file drawers, cabinets with doors, or storage units for a particular kind of library material. The shape of the desk can be a functional consideration if the staff plans to have other tasks or activities take place in the same area.

The most important maintenance considerations involve the worksurface of the desk. The top should be covered with a material that does not get marred when heavy materials and equipment are dragged across or dropped upon it. The surface should be one that can be cleaned easily on a daily basis. Ideally, the desk top will be constructed in such a manner that the top only can be replaced. The staff might want to note that neither the cabinet nor the top of the desk should have sharp edges that can be easily damaged.

As with the other items in the building, the style, finish, and design of the desk should also be considered in regard to appearance. Because the circulation desk is often the first thing that is seen by patrons entering the library, the desk's appearance plays an important role in creating a first impression. The design should, therefore, be inviting, and the function of the desk should be immediately apparent. While the desk should be a distinctive element in the building, it should not be so monumental that users are reluctant to approach staff working there.

All of the considerations in regard to the circulation desk are applicable to the reference desk as well. While the functions are different, the staff will consider similar factors in describing reference area needs. They might want to have a worksurface 29″ high and a transaction top across the front of the desk 39″ to 42″ high. Different libraries will require different types of storage behind the reference desk. Some libraries will require special accommodations for ready-reference material of various types. A wire management system will probably be needed. Some tasks done at the circulation desk in one library may be carried out at the reference desk in another. Also, in small libraries, one desk may be used for both circulation and reference for some—or all—of the time.

Early discussions about the function of the shelving to be selected should center around anticipated amounts and kinds of materials to be stored. In an academic library, book storage will probably involve storing large numbers of books as efficiently as possible. In a school or public library, bookstacks will be needed for picture books, for children's fiction and nonfiction, and for adult books. There may also be a need for book and audio-visual display shelving. A special library may require heavy-duty shelving for large volumes and specialized storage

for other kinds of materials. Many libraries will require shelving for periodicals as well as books.

Maintenance considerations for shelving for a public library might involve the following:

> *Maintenance.* We want bookstacks that have shelves that can be moved easily from section to section as the library changes. The shelving should be easy to assemble and disassemble, if we want to move the ranges some day. Specialized hardware should not be required in order to keep the shelving stable. The shelving should be so well-made that it remains stable even though it is moved several times. The parts of the shelving should be interchangeable, so we can adapt it to changing conditions. There should be some way of leveling the shelving easily. The finish on the shelving should not nick or scratch easily.

In many libraries, appearance is not going to be the primary factor to consider when selecting shelving. While the staff of a small public or school library might prefer the look of wooden shelving, budget constraints may force it to consider steel shelving, or steel shelving with wooden end panels. In the closed-stack areas of most libraries, function and maintenance will be the important factors to consider; appearance will have very little to do with the selection of the shelving.

Similarly, with lateral or vertical files, microform storage, etc., function and maintenance will be more important factors than appearance. For example, there are many attractive lateral or vertical files; therefore, the staff should describe the files needed in terms of function and maintenance: files should store the materials efficiently, be safe to use when fully loaded, have drawers that open and close satisfactorily with heavy use, have parts that can be replaced or repaired, withstand moving from place to place, and have a finish that is not easily marred.

The information compiled in this process is, in effect, the furniture program to be used when selecting specific products. As noted earlier, in many situations the parties involved may be so familiar with the needs of the library that no formal process like the one described above will be necessary. Whether or not the process results in a written document, however, the thought process is necessary in order to ensure that the librarian, or others involved in the selection, can speak confidently and intelligibly to suppliers.

The process establishes the level of quality to be expected in the building interior when it is completed. Decisions made early in the project may ensure that the furnishings purchased will continue to be useful and attractive for many years to come.

The obvious question at this point is: What about the money? Does the library have the funds to purchase the quality of furnishings desired? That question will be answered as the librarian begins the next step in the decision-making process, which is to seek information about what is available.

The price of a product is based upon many factors, including the quality and cost of the materials used, the quality of workmanship that goes into making it, the volume of sales, competition in the marketplace, and whether the item is a standard or customized product for that manufacturer. Because there are several products that will fulfill the needs and wants of most libraries, it is advisable to study the advertising literature and talk to the vendors of several different products.

Here is a scenario that might take place: the representative of Company A says the company can provide just what is wanted, but the representative knows the requested item will have to be custom-made by the manufacturer. Company B, on the other hand, may be able to supply the item as a standard product. In that case, Company B will offer a better price because the product can be manufactured for less.

It is also important to remember that the initial expenditure should be viewed in terms of the cost to the library over the number of years the piece will be used. In the long run, a less expensive item may cost the library more, in terms of total dollars, if it has a fairly short life span and has to be replaced or repaired more quickly.

Having gone through the process of deciding what the library would ideally like to have, the librarian should be able to describe rather accurately to vendors what is desired in terms of level of quality, function, appearance, etc. Based on this information, vendors should be able to provide some ballpark estimates of the price of their products. If it is immediately evident that the first-choice product is too expensive, salespeople will be willing to offer alternatives that will provide a similar level of quality without the refinements or extras that the luxury item has. Compromise is often necessary on matters that deal strictly with appearance. A librarian may choose to give up some stylistic elements in particular pieces in order to get a higher level of quality in other items. Because of the electrical requirements of the circulation and catalog areas, for example, a librarian may buy standard leg-base tables and less expensive reading chairs, so that funds will be available to purchase a circulation desk and computer workstations that contain a top-of-the-line electrical system.

When talking to vendors, it is important to keep several things in mind. First, no single manufacturer or supplier can do everything. Be wary of a salesperson who claims to be able to supply anything needed or wanted, regardless of materials used, construction, or amount of funds available. Also, if a vendor says prices will be revealed or needed product information provided only if the librarian promises to let her/him "do the job," that vendor is asking too much. While vendors cannot be expected to spend a lot of time figuring exact prices at this point, they should be able to provide enough information for the librarian to know whether or not the product falls within the budget. (A more in-depth discussion of the vendor's responsibilities will be found in Chapter 11.)

In addition to gathering information about specific products, the librarian should also ask and have answered these questions about the supplier:

1. How long has the vendor been in business?
2. How long has the vendor been selling the product being considered?
3. Who manufactures the product?
4. How long has the manufacturer been in business?
5. Who will do the installation of the product?
6. Is the installer familiar with the product?
7. What delivery time can be expected for the product?
8. Has the vendor/manufacturer/installer done other projects similar in scope to the one now planned?
9. Who will be responsible for following up on the project once the installation is complete; i.e., who will handle problems that might arise later?
10. What are the warranties and guarantees offered on the products and labor supplied?

While the length of time a vendor has been in business does not provide any insurance for the future, a company that has been in existence for several years can provide a list of references of successfully completed projects that have stood up over time. Obviously, the longer a vendor has sold the product, or a similar one, the more s/he should know about it. A list of references should be carefully checked to see if the earlier projects were similar in scope to the current one, and to determine whether or not the products, installation, and service provided were satisfactory.

Do not assume that the name on the product reveals who actually manufactures the item. For example, while most library supply houses include steel shelving products in their catalogs, not all of them own a manufacturing plant. Several companies purchase a product from another manufacturer and sell it under their brand name. It might be cheaper to buy directly from the manufacturer than to buy from the supplier. Also, knowing its manufacturer may tell you more about the product if the manufacturer has an established reputation.

In some cases, it is not only important to know how long the manufacturer has been in business, but how long the current owner has held the company. Product quality sometimes changes as owners change, even though the name of the company stays the same. For that reason, it is best not to assume that because Brand A was an unreliable product ten years ago, it should not be considered now, or vice versa. Furniture or shelving made by a company that has changed ownership should be evaluated like any new product, on the basis of the specific criteria to be discussed in later chapters.

Some products require installation by someone who is factory-trained. In any case, the installer should be familiar with the product, or the kind of product. In large projects, it is obviously very important to ascertain whether the manufacturer, the supplier, and the installer have successfully handled jobs of the size planned, because occasionally a company will bid on a job that is outside the scope of its capabilities in terms of quantities needed, delivery time expected, type of construction desired, etc. In that case, the librarian who has not investigated could be left with late delivery or quality below that specified.

The best way to get to know a company is to tour its factory. When a manufacturer is interested in a large library project, it is not unusual for some of the decision makers in the selection process to be invited by the company to visit the plant. Here are some observations to make and questions to ask when visiting a wood furniture manufacturer:

1. Notice how the raw materials are handled. Some companies are more involved than others in the quality control of the wood used. Library Bureau, for example, has a saw mill and actually cuts some of the wood from logs at the factory; Buckstaff grades and dries its own lumber and maintains close quality control on the materials used.
2. Take a close look at the detail and craftsmanship of items being produced in the factory. The representative of a company that prides itself on quality will point out distinctive features of construction and appearance while you are touring the plant.
3. Notice whether the company is using several different types of materials, three-ply flakeboard and five-ply lumber core, for example, and whether custom as well as stock items are in production.
4. Look for evidence of quality control. Are finished items checked carefully before they are shipped? Are large pieces, such as circulation desks, assembled at the plant before they are shipped to make sure that the components of the finished product are constructed according to the drawings and that all of the parts fit together correctly?
5. Ask about performance testing of products and take a look at any in-house testing facility. Does the information given about products show evidence that the company has engineered its furniture to last?
6. Is the management interested in getting input about new product needs from the librarian? Is the company involved in new product development?
7. Is the company interested in marketing and concerned about providing adequate support for its representatives in the field?

There are several ways to purchase library furnishings. In most cases, the purchase is handled on a bid basis, so that suppliers are competing against each other. In this situation, the purchaser is dependent upon the vendor to provide a price determined by the conditions of the particular job. The name of the dealer or manufacturer's representative for the area can be obtained by calling the company headquarters. (The addresses and phone numbers of many of the manufacturers discussed in the following chapters can be found at the back of the book.) Furnishings can also be purchased from a catalog at a list price. While this may be viewed as an easy way to handle the purchase, it is not the best way to obtain a competitive price, nor does this method necessarily allow the buyer to ask questions about the product and specify exactly what quality is demanded. In some situations, a library may put out a request for proposals (RFP) and, in effect, negotiate the job with the vendors. Regardless of the purchase method used, the librarian should talk with each prospective supplier, ask questions about the construction of the product, obtain written specifications, and ask for the names of libraries using the supplier's product for more than a year.

In summary, the librarian or others involved in making decisions about furnishings need to ask many questions. In order to be able to ask the right questions and make an informed decision, knowledge of what assures quality in a product is needed. The following chapters provide information to help you evaluate product quality.

Chapter 3
Elements of Quality Construction

The Effect of Liability and Standards on the Market

One of the primary motivations for making educated decisions in the selection of furnishings is the desire to get the most for your money. Librarians as a group are a major market for several manufacturers and can, therefore, have an effect on the industry standard, if they demand a certain level of quality in products and services. One of the characteristics that distinguishes some manufacturers/vendors from others is the degree to which they are customer-responsive; i.e., how interested they are in providing products that have the qualities of function, maintenance, and appearance desired in the library.

While an increased librarian interest in improving interiors has prompted some responsiveness from manufacturers, another motivating factor in their responsiveness has been the matter of product liability. An excellent discussion of this subject is presented in *Specifications for Commercial Interiors; Professional Liabilities, Regulations, and Performance Criteria* by S. C. Reznikoff (1979). Reznikoff defines product liability as follows:

> Product liability is primarily concerned with negligence. It is considered the "duty" of the manufacturer to provide products that will not expose the consumer to undue risk, bodily injury, death or property damage as a result of the construction, design, installation, and assembly of the product. Also included in product liability actions is the manufacturer's failure to ward against a danger or hazard in the use or misuse of the product and failure to provide adequate instructions for the use of the product. Violation of *express warranty* may also be involved. An express warranty is a guaranty of performance and includes all advertising claims made by the manufacturer. (p.17)

Like architects, designers, and manufacturers of contract office furniture, some library furnishings manufacturers have reacted to the increase in product liability lawsuits by increasing performance testing and by complying with industry standards and codes, as well as with governmental regulations. Librarians who specify products that meet the more stringent standards, who support their specifications, and who then insist on purchasing products that meet these specs, are giving a message to manufacturers that this is the level of quality expected by the library market.

Performance tests and many codes and standards are highly technical and often difficult to interpret. The consumer should question vendors as to how well their products meet the standards and whether or not certain items have been performance-tested. The real leaders in the industry are interested in complying with the standards and have performance-tested their products. Any vendor should be able to provide data that can be compared to similar information from other companies.

One possible scenario is that Company A will be responsive to a particular standard; Company B will then tell the consumer that since its product is the same as the one made by Company A, Company B doesn't need to do the testing. As a sales technique, this works only if the consumer does not understand the rationale behind the standard, and is willing to take the word of the salesperson for the technical details involved in compliance with the standard.

A specific example of this situation follows: The Worden Company led library furniture manufacturers in going through the expensive and time-consuming process of getting its electrical system, as a unit, listed by the Underwriters Laboratories for meeting the UL1286 *Standard for Safety* (to be discussed in more detail below). As the only library furniture manufacturer complying with UL1286 guidelines, Worden achieved product differentiation because it was the only company truly meeting specifications when the UL1286 standard was required in a bid document. Compliance also gave the company protection from possible liability suits.

In the meantime, many other manufacturers also introduced some kind of electrical system into their own product lines. Representatives of some of those companies have, however, downplayed or ignored the necessity of complying with UL1286 in selling, and have, on occasion, said compliance is not necessary because the system sold by their company is the same as that manufactured by Worden. The assertion may or may not be true, but since the standards change frequently and are extremely detailed, the consumer may be accepting a lot on faith in believing this claim.

Several other library furniture manufacturers have now taken steps toward complying with UL1286. For the sake of the consumer, as well as the industry, all companies should do whatever is necessary to bring their electrical systems into compliance with the most stringent standards. (Many manufacturers of office panel systems, by the way, have been complying with these standards for some time.) Libraries would then benefit from lower prices in bid situations, if several companies comply with the same high standards in their electrical systems. There would also be more choice for selection of a brand with the same level of quality, and libraries would be protected from possible liability suits. Finally, since products could no longer be differentiated on the basis of their electrical systems, library manufacturers would be forced to look for additional improvements or changes, which could result in further advantages for the consumer.

Power Distribution and Wire Management*

In *Specifications for Commercial Interiors*, S. C. Reznikoff points out that designers can minimize product liability actions by specifying products manufactured for the intended use. This is one of the reasons manufacturers have sought compliance with the UL1286 standards explained below. The companies are ensuring their own protection from liability suits which can result from improper use of electrical components in furniture.

Underwriters Laboratories (UL) is an independent testing agency. The American National Standards Institute (ANSI) adopted UL1286 as its national standard for the use of electrical equipment in furniture. In addition, the standards of the National Electrical Code (NEC) have been raised to a level closer to that established by UL1286.

Many librarians will not care to study the standards in great detail. For most purposes, it is sufficient to know that the UL1286 standards address electrical safety, the stability of furniture, and the flammability of furniture. Compliance in regard to electrical safety includes standards for the types and lengths of cords and conduit that can be used in particular situations, the manner in which outlets are mounted and in which cords pass through panels, the type of connectors and plug configurations to be

used in certain applications, the materials that are used in the components, and the way in which power entry into the furniture is accomplished.

Most, if not all, library furniture manufacturers have various pieces of their electrical systems that are UL recognized; that is, the items either meet appropriate standards or have been tested and found suitable for use in a particular manner. Compliance with UL1286, however, requires that the components as a *working unit* are listed and, therefore, can be used safely together. Also, a manufacturer who has a product that is in compliance with UL1286 is subject to quarterly inspections by UL after the initial investigation to ensure that the materials and construction continue to comply with the standards.

There are several ways for a consumer to determine whether an electrical system complies with UL1286. First, a product thus manufactured can be identified by the UL labeling on a specific piece of furniture, such as a carrel, which states: "Office Furnishing by Company A For Use With Listed Office Furnishing Accessories by Company A." A second electrical label will be on any accessory (an electrical component, such as a raceway, that is intended to be attached in the field, or may be shipped separately). The label on the accessory will state: "Office Furnishing Accessory by Company A For Use With Listed Office Furnishings By Company A." Both labels include the UL file number (beginning with the letter E-) which identifies the particular manufacturer. Because the UL1286 standard involves the use of components within a system, compliance requires a company to supply assembly manuals with its products. Both mechanical and electrical instructions are required to ensure that all of the elements can be put together correctly in the field. In a bid document, then, when furniture is required to have an electrical system that complies with UL1286, the specifications can state that the vendor is required to supply assembly manuals for the products. The status of a product can also be verified by calling Underwriters Laboratories.

Several companies now have a wire management system. The most basic systems have grommets in the desk or table top that provide access to a J-shaped channel, mounted below the worksurface, for carrying cables and cords to the power supply. (A grommet is a plastic or metal ring that fits into a hole to protect cords running through the opening.) A second electrical component that is becoming standard is the metal wireway that is mounted in or on a worksurface and provides convenient access to outlets located in the wireway. (See Figure 4). The systems typically offer modular single or multi-circuit options. The single-circuit systems terminate

---

*This section is based heavily on information supplied by Robert Boardman of The Worden Company in conversations and in his publications.

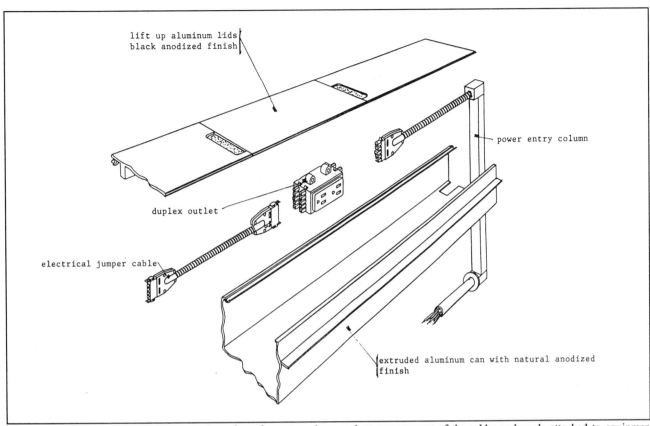

lift up aluminum lids
black anodized finish

power entry column

duplex outlet

electrical jumper cable

extruded aluminum can with natural anodized finish

Figure 4. A satisfactory electrical system allows for safe, neat, and convenient management of the cables and cords attached to equipment used on the worksurface of a table or desk. *Drawing courtesy of The Worden Company.*

at the power entry point with a 20-amp, three-pronged, grounded plug. It is important to note that the 20-amp offset configuration plug cannot be used in a standard 15-amp receptacle. (See Figure 5). Architects and engineers working on building projects need to know when the library will be using equipment so designed. Two- and three-circuit systems must be hardwired to the building's power supply by a qualified, licensed electrician. The multi-circuit systems allow for designating a circuit for computer use.

Another consideration in the electrical system is the availability of adequate built-in surge suppression devices. Several kinds are available. In order to obtain the best kind in a given situation, the vendor should be asked to explain in layperson's terms how the surge suppression device will protect the particular equipment to be used. From the standpoint of the flexibility of the system and for aesthetic reasons, a final consideration is the manner in which power entry into the item of furniture is accomplished. Some systems have a wood chase that carries the power into an item with a panel base. Worden, the forerunner in the field, also offers a power leg on wooden furnishings and power entry through the hollow metal leg of the Diametron series.

In summary, the following questions should be asked and answered in regard to the electrical sys-

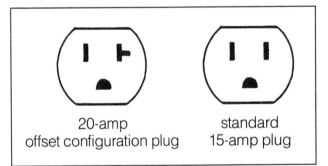

20-amp
offset configuration plug

standard
15-amp plug

Figure 5. The 20-amp three-pronged, grounded plug used on some single-circuit electrical systems cannot be plugged into a standard 15-amp receptacle.

tem to be used in tables, carrels, reference and circulation desks, etc.:

1. Is the electrical system UL1286 listed? Does it comply with the National Electrical Code or any applicable local codes?

2. Does the wire management system keep the worksurface free of cables and cords except at the point where the cords enter the wireway?

3. Does the system allow for cords to enter the wireway at many points along the worksurface, so that the use of space can be adjusted as needs change?

4. Does the wire management system keep the space below the work surface as neat as the area above?
5. How adaptable is the system? Does it allow for neat and unobtrusive entry of power, datalines, etc., into the piece of equipment, regardless of the design of the furniture?
6. Can the wireway be locked? Is the system designed to be relatively tamper-free if it is to be used in a public reading area?
7. Does each piece of equipment—for example, a double-faced row of carrels—allow for powering the entire unit from only one point (if all pieces of equipment to be used on the item can be safely used on the circuits provided)?
8. Does the system have built-in surge protection?
9. Does the system provide for special electrical needs, such as isolated grounded circuits?

Questions that should be brought to the attention of the architect or others involved in a building project include:

1. Will some of the items require hardwiring? Which items will require a 20-amp receptacle? Has the architect been apprised of the electrical requirements of the furnishings?
2. Has the use of flatwire and carpet tiles, rather than conduit, been considered in the building project?
3. Have power locations in the building been coordinated with the power entry points on the individual pieces of furniture?
4. Have enough circuits been provided to allow for safe use of the necessary equipment? (To answer this, the librarian must inform the architect which pieces of equipment will be used on each item of furniture now, and what other items might be used there in the future.)

No attempt has been made here to go into detail about the specific standards for electrical systems, because, as in all of the other topics discussed here, changes occur so frequently that the information would quickly be out-of-date. The consumer is encouraged, once again, to ask lots of questions of reliable vendors, consultants, and architects.

Wood Construction

Most fine-quality library furniture is constructed of wood. It is essential when selecting furnishings, therefore, to have some background knowledge of wood and wood products, joinery, construction, and wood finishes. The actual construction of a piece of wood furniture cannot necessarily be determined by looking at the finished product. What may look like a solid piece of wood may actually be a veneer, a thin slice of wood used to face a core of another kind of material. For this reason it may be risky to purchase inexpensive furniture from an office supply catalog; the information given may be incomplete or misleading. A $200 desk may look fine when it's purchased, but don't expect it to provide the library the same use over a period of years as an $800 desk. The primary decision to be made by the purchaser in regard to wood furniture is which kind of construction to select. Wood library furniture is constructed of three-ply flakeboard or particleboard, five-ply lumber core, eighteen- or nineteen-ply wood core, solid butcher block, and solid wood plank.

One of the best sources of information about wood used in furnishings is *Architectural Woodwork Quality Standards, Guide Specifications and Quality Certification Program*, published by the Architectural Woodwork Institute (AWI). According to AWI, flakeboard or particleboard is "manufactured from natural wood reduced to particles, fibers, or chips mixed with binders, and formed by the use of heat and pressure into panels." (p. 22) Most high-quality flakeboard used in furniture is medium density, that is, 45 lbs. per cubic foot. The term *three-ply* refers to the particleboard core and the face and back veneers (or the plastic laminate and backing) that are applied to it.

Lumber core consists of strips of kiln-dried wood, often common poplar, basswood, or aspen, of random widths (usually from 2½″ to 4″ wide) and lengths which are edge-glued into panels. Crossbands of wood running in the opposite direction of the grain of the lumber core are then placed on either side of the core. Finally, face and back veneers (with the grain running parallel to the core and the opposite direction of the crossbands) are applied to make up the five plies. Butcher block construction involves the use of solid staves or narrow strips of wood which are face-glued. Wood plank is also occasionally used in the form of solid edge-glued panels. (See Figures 6A-D).

Manufacturers and vendors offer consumers differing opinions on the quality of construction that is possible using particleboard, lumber core, or butcher block. Usually, a company line is based to a great extent on the material selected for use in their standard product. For example, some companies use solid lumber core tops on all of their tables as a standard, and claim this decision was made because of the desire to make the best available product. Other manufacturers, however, use a flakeboard or particleboard core as standard construction material, and have performance-tested their products regularly to demonstrate the reliability of this material. Most of the major library manufacturers will now build in either three-ply flakeboard or five-ply lumber core, depending on what the purchaser specifies. Likewise, they will selectively use solid lumber rather than flakeboard in different parts of the same items, if function demands it. For example, most companies

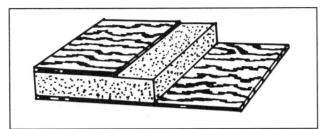

Figure 6A. Three-ply construction consists of a particleboard core plus face and back veneers (or plastic laminate and backing).

Figure 6B. Five-ply construction includes a lumber core, two crossbands running in the opposite direction of the grain of the core, and face and back veneers with the grain running parallel to the core.

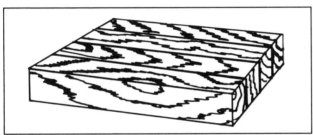

Figure 6C. Butcher block consists of narrow strips of wood that are face-glued.

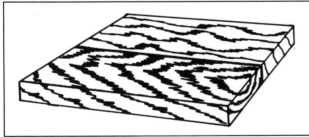

Figure 6D. Wood plank is used in the form of solid edge-glued panels.

place high-pressure laminate table tops over a particleboard core. Some companies offer the option of butcher block or solid wood plank in addition to using the other materials.

Selection of wood furnishings does not necessarily involve answering the question of which type of construction to choose. Rather, particleboard, lumber core, and solid wood are all reasonable choices with advantages and disadvantages to be weighed in deciding which material to specify. Robert Boardman (1981) points out some of the factors to be weighed in selecting particleboard versus lumber core construction. He notes that one of the major

disadvantages of working with wood in any form is the ability of this natural material to absorb moisture from the atmosphere. "The most important development with regard to the control of hygroscopic expansion and shrinkage of furniture panels is the cross-lamination of wood," that is, applying the layers of wood so that the grain of a layer is at a right angle to the grain of the ply below it. Cross-lamination is only advantageous if the plies are perfectly balanced. The plies on opposite sides of the core must be of the same thickness, moisture content, and species, in order to avoid warping of lumber core panels.

There are two major advantages to five-ply lumber core construction: (1) form stability, or the structural strength to withstand long-term loading, and (2) a solid edge that can be shaped and finished, and that provides good holding power for mechanical fasteners on the edge grain. Particleboard, however, is less expensive, and has some other advantages over lumber core or butcher block. For example, particleboard has more dimensional stability; it has greater "resistance to linear and thickness expansion or shrinkage of a panel as a result of changes of the wood moisture content." If the materials on either side of the core are balanced correctly, there is less likelihood of warping of a particleboard than a lumber core panel.

The most frequently mentioned disadvantage to particleboard is its screw-holding power. "Screws driven into the edges of particle board have a screw-holding power considerably less than that of solid wood, while the screw-holding power on the face of the board is entirely satisfactory. Usually, in order to increase the edge screw-holding power, the particle board edges must be reinforced with solid wood members." (Boardman, 1981) Other factors that affect the satisfactory use of particleboard construction are the density of the particleboard, the sizes of the screws used in the construction, backer sheets used, and any other components that go into making the panel.

In summary, either particleboard or lumber core can be considered a satisfactory material for constructing library furniture. If funds are available, parts of tables, shelving, or chairs that are important to the structural strength or stability of the item will ideally be constructed of lumber core. Items like end panels for steel shelving, which are added mainly for the sake of appearance, can be constructed of the less expensive particleboard. A library that makes the economical choice of purchasing furniture constructed almost totally of particleboard can be assured of having a satisfactory product for most uses, if the items are made by a reliable manufacturer.

In the future, consumers may have to consider another factor in selecting core material. Some stringent flammability standards now require evidence that core material used in furnishings is fireproof.

Such regulations may force the consumer to specify, for example, particleboard rather than lumber core, if the former has greater fire retardant capabilities.

Most manufacturers use northern-grown red oak for face veneers and in their standard products where solid wood is specified, as in the edge bands of tables, shelves, and stabilizing keels. The wood is kiln-dried to an acceptable moisture content of between 5 percent and 7 percent. When a finish other than natural oak is desired, the wood is often stained to simulate the color of other woods, such as mahogany or cherry. If the consumer is willing to pay the price, most manufacturers will also work with solid woods other than oak on special projects.

The finished look of a piece of high-quality furniture is often determined by the face veneer used. Face veneers used by domestic manufacturers are usually no less than 1/28″ thick. The appearance of the grain in different types of veneer is the result of the way in which a log segment is cut with relation to the annual rings. (See Figure 7). Veneer cuts include the following:

> *Rotary:* As the name implies, the log is mounted in a lathe and cut against a blade, like unwinding a roll of paper. A bold grain figure is produced.
>
> *Rift-cut:* Produced from "various species of oak. Oak has medullary ray cells which radiate from the center of the log like the spokes of a wheel. The rift is obtained by slicing slightly across these medullary rays. This accentuates the vertical grain."
>
> *Plain or flat slicing:* The half-log is sliced parallel to a line through the center of the log. The grain figure is similar to that of plain sawn lumber.
>
> *Half-round slicing:* Logs are mounted off-center in the lathe, so that the result has some of the characteristics of both rotary- and plain-sliced veneers.
>
> *Quarter slicing:* The quarter-log is sliced so that the growth rings of the log strike the blade at approximately right angles, making the grain show as a series of stripes.

Other visual aspects of the veneer are the result of the way in which the individual pieces of veneer, called "leaves," are arranged or matched. Most matching is done with sliced, rather than rotary cut, veneers. (See Figure 8). Matching between adjacent veneer leaves includes the following:

> *End-matching:* "leaves are book-matched end to end as well as side to side."
>
> *Slip-matching:* "adjoining leaves are slipped out in sequence [as they were cut from the log], with all the same face sides being exposed."

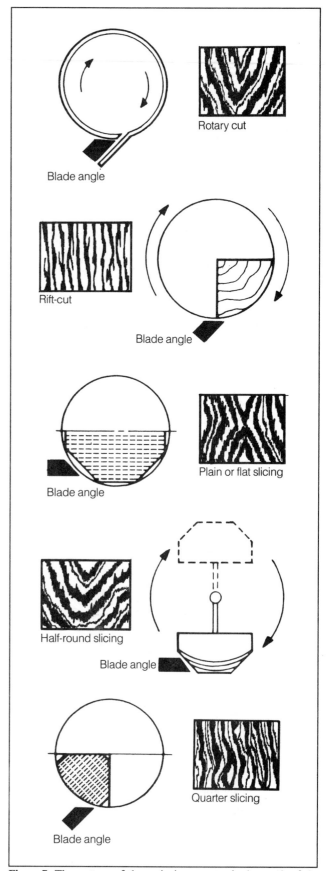

Figure 7. The pattern of the grain in a veneer is the result of the way in which a log segment is cut with relation to the annual rings.

Book-matching: "Every other piece of veneer is turned over, so that adjacent leaves are 'opened' as two pages in a book." The visual effect is that "veneer joints match, creating a symmetrical pattern." Book-matching within a panel may be a running match in which "each panel face is assembled from as many veneer leaves as necessary"; a balance match in which "each panel face is assembled from leaves of uniform width"; or a center match in which "each panel has an even number of veneer leaves of uniform width. Thus, there is a veneer joint in the center of the panel, producing horizontal symmetry."

Random-matching: The arrangement of the leaves from one or more logs resulting in a casual, boardlike effect.

(Quoted definitions are from *Architectural Woodwork Quality Standards,* pp. 25–27.)

Library furnishings manufacturers do not use as their standard the same cuts of veneer or match. Library Bureau and Buckstaff, for example, use slip-matching as standard, while Worden panels are book-matched.

While the type of veneer used has an effect on the appearance of the furniture, the more important maintenance consideration is the finish that is placed on the wood. Almost any finish will look good on a new piece of furniture, but what happens after it has been used for years? *Architectural Woodwork Quality Standards* includes a detailed chart (p. 114) that compares the performance data on a number of wood-finishing systems. The best overall finishes for wood, from the standpoint of durability and maintenance, are *catalyzed* (not standard nitrocellulose) lacquer or conversion alkyd-urea varnish. Parts of furnishings that are subjected to extraordinary wear, such as wide edge bands on carrels, can be made even more durable by the use of a catalyzed polyurethane finish. Polyester resin and epoxy resin are also used as wood finishes. While these are used on horizontal surfaces in places other than libraries—in restaurants, for example—there is not enough evidence available to demonstrate their reliability on public worksurfaces in the library. They can be used to provide an attractive finish for vertical surfaces, however.

High-pressure laminates are frequently preferred over veneers as facing materials for wood. The standard laminates used on furnishings are .050″ thick for horizontal surfaces and .028″ thick for vertical surfaces. A backing .020″ thick is used to balance the construction. While a manufacturer may maintain a supply of certain laminates as part of its standard product line, a purchaser can specify a laminate from the lines of any of the major suppliers, such as Formica, Wilsonart, and Nevamar.

In addition to the basic materials used to construct and finish wood furniture, the manner in which the item is put together contributes to the quality of the product. The use of appropriate joints, or joinery, between the various parts of the furniture can add to the strength and appearance of the item.

When talking to vendors or reading manufacturers' specifications, it is helpful to understand the following terms used in wood construction (See Figure 9 for illustrations):

Butt joint: The easiest method for joining two pieces of wood, by simply butting them together at a 90-degree angle, without intermembering the two pieces. This is not a very strong joint until it is reinforced in some manner.

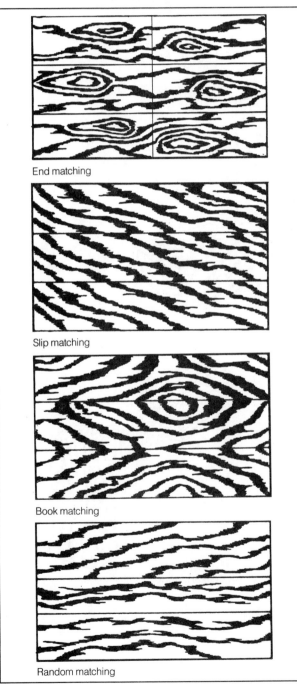

End matching

Slip matching

Book matching

Random matching

Figure 8. A veneer match is the result of the specific way in which the individual pieces of veneer, called leaves, are arranged.

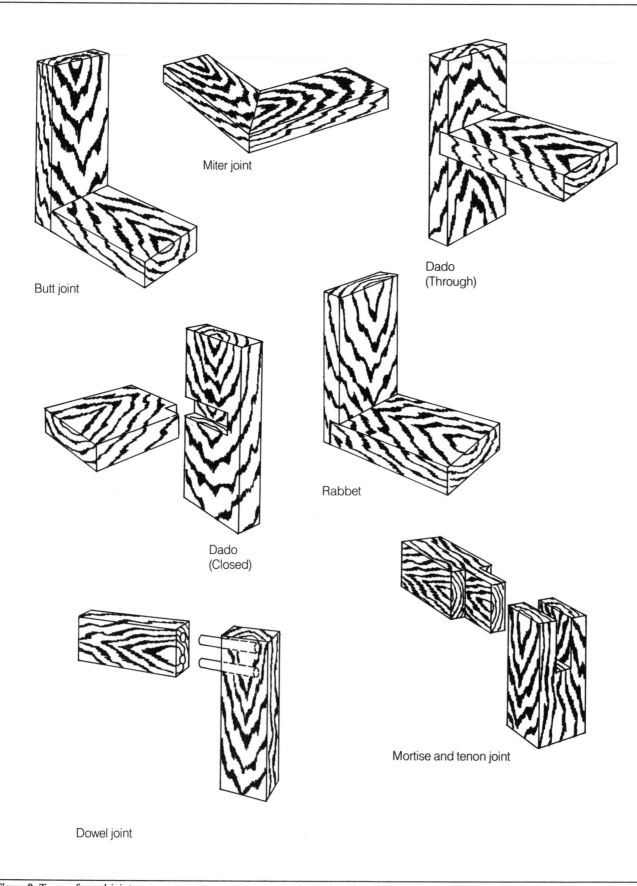

Figure 9. Types of wood joints.

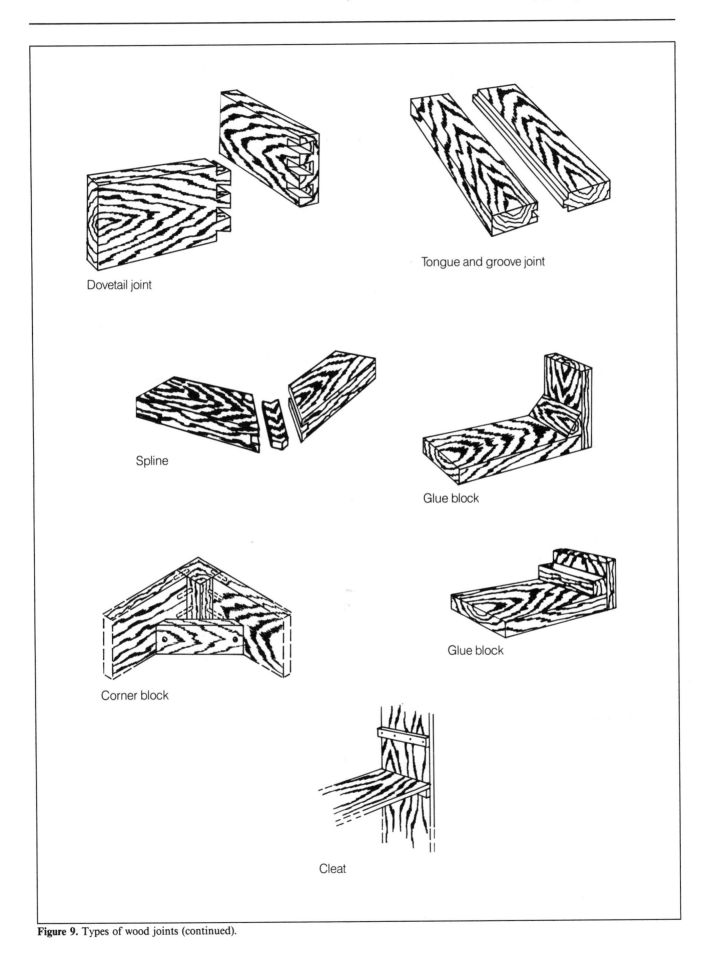

Figure 9. Types of wood joints (continued).

Miter joint: A joint in which the two pieces are cut at an angle. On a square corner, for example, each piece of wood will be cut at a 45-degree angle, to form a 90-degree angle. Mitered corners are used to give a finished look to a high-quality piece of furniture.

Dado: A rectangular groove cut into the face of a piece of wood, and into which a second piece of wood can be inserted. In a through dado, the groove goes all the way across the face of the wood. In a blind, closed, or stop dado, the groove partially crosses the board. The dado is used to join parts of a cabinet or bookcase.

Rabbet: An L-shaped groove cut along the edge of a piece of wood, which then intermembers with the edge of a second piece of wood. It is used to attach the fronts to drawers, backs to cabinets, etc.

Dowel joint: Any joint that is reinforced by inserting dowels (round wooden pegs) into holes on the inside of the two pieces of wood to be joined. Dowel joints are used, for example, to join the rails of chairs to the legs.

Mortise and tenon joint: A mortise is a hole or notch made in a piece of wood, into which a tenon, a piece of wood of the same dimension, is placed. The joint can be a blind mortise and tenon, which *looks* like a butt joint, or an open mortise and tenon, which is a strong, attractive joint used to join two parts of a chair arm or a chair rail to the leg.

Dovetail joint: Essentially a mortise and tenon joint, in which the tenon is broader at the end than at the base. The two pieces of wood are joined like interlocking fingers. Dovetail joints are used mainly in drawer construction. Fine card catalog drawers are made with dovetail joints.

Tongue and groove joint: A joint used to join the *edges* of two pieces of wood. As the name implies, a groove is cut out of the edge of one piece of wood, so it will intermember with another piece of wood that has a tongue, or raised edge, of the same dimension.

Spline: A narrow strip of wood used to join two pieces of wood, the edges of which have been grooved to receive the spline. These are used to reinforce a miter joint.

Glue block: Small blocks of wood used to reinforce a frame that is supporting a horizontal surface such as a chair seat or table top.

Corner block: A triangular piece of wood, larger than a glue block, which is used to reinforce a corner joint in a chair or table where the legs and side rails meet.

Cleat: A block of wood used to support a shelf or other piece of wood.

While several library manufacturers are capable of making high-quality furnishings, the attention to detail in the design and the overall workmanship

apparent in the finished item distinguish some products from others. Many consumers are so accustomed to accepting less than the best that they do not know what can reasonably be expected from a reliable manufacturer. When evaluating a line of wood furniture, a librarian can get a better idea of how the items function by looking at the furnishings in a library setting, rather than in a booth at a conference. While many specific features about tables, chairs, and other furnishings will be discussed in the following chapters, these are examples of the kinds of general questions to ask or details to consider about wood furniture:

1. Do all parts of an item fit together snugly? There should not be a gap, for example, between the worksurface and the side of a study carrel, or between a shelf on a double-tiered index table and the end panel, or between the sections of a modular circulation desk.

2. Look at anything that contains a shelf. Is there any indication of the shelf bending in the middle from the load? Are empty shelves level or do they appear to be warped slightly? Is the shelf pulling away from the sides? How is each shelf supported?

3. Consider how the edges are finished. Are there attractive wood edge bands that fit snugly against the sides and that are flush with the surface? Are wide edge bands mitered on the corners? Do the miters fit together snugly?

4. Are plastic laminates flush with edge bands? Do long worksurfaces (like those on a circulation desk) have continuous tops, so there are very few seams between pieces of laminate?

5. Are veneers matched in some fashion? Is the color of various items consistent? Has the finish remained in good condition, even on areas that receive heavy wear, such as on the edges of tables or the arms of chairs?

6. Do drawers open and close easily? Do cabinet doors fit well when they are closed?

7. Are there attractive details in the construction that indicate craftsmanship went into the design? For example, can you see open mortise and tenon joinery, dovetail joints in drawers, finished surfaces on the working, as well as public, side of desks?

While manufacturers understandably prefer to make their standard products, they are equipped to make modifications to accommodate some unusual function or to make a project distinctive. Although these modifications or special designs are more expensive, there is no harm in discussing the possibility with a vendor. It is quite common for manufacturers to do some customizing on any job that involves providing furniture for a new building.

Chapter 4
Shelving

As long as books continue to be the primary information source in libraries, shelving is the most important item to be selected in a building or renovation project. Shelving is used to organize, store, and display the major product to be marketed in the library. For this reason, the decisions concerning what type of shelving to choose and which brand to purchase are crucial to the success of the building. High-quality bookstacks will last the lifetime of the library. The best shelving available for the funds allocated should be selected, and can be considered a long-term investment.

While stability and strength are vital to a library planning to use the shelving for years, the liability factor involved in the safe use of shelving makes the selection of bookstacks even more critical. Librarians are well aware of the real possibility of lawsuits resulting from loaded bookstacks that fall and injure, or even kill, someone.

Most libraries choose wood bookstacks, cantilevered steel shelving, or a similar product that is gaining popularity, a steel shelving system with wood end panels. Most of the information given below will relate to these three types of shelving. Because all kinds of libraries are now using compact shelving systems, the last part of the chapter will discuss some of these products.

In addition to the three styles of shelving noted above, several others are marketed as library bookstacks. Some companies that manufacture industrial shelving, for example, sell a post-lock or four-post type of shelving to the library market. Library Bureau, Aurora, and Montel are three of these companies. Post-lock shelving is sometimes used in compact shelving systems. For the most part, however, this type of shelving is used in industrial or warehouse situations.

Multi-tier steel bookstacks and case-style shelving of steel, or a combination of steel and wood, are also sold to libraries. Multi-tier has typically been used in academic installations, where the quantity of book storage needed is so large that it is cheaper to purchase multi-tier shelving than to construct several floors with the load-bearing requirements needed for fully loaded bookstacks. Library Bureau and Aetnastack are manufacturers of multi-tier systems.

Case-style shelving is sometimes used by libraries that want the look of wood library shelving in a less expensive form. This shelving is more apt to be used in offices and special libraries than in public or academic libraries. For example, it is used in law libraries where the size of the volumes is fairly uniform, and there is little need to adjust the distance between shelves or to interfile volumes of all different sizes on the same shelf. A case-style bookstack, named Adjustable Shelving, is manufactured by Supreme Equipment and Systems Corporation. Russ Bassett and Adjustable Steel Products Company make a case-type bookstack that has steel shelves in a wood case. (Some other wood/steel systems made specifically for libraries are discussed following the section on steel shelving.)

When choosing shelving, one of the three selection factors (function, maintenance, or appearance) is likely to be an overriding consideration in making the decision. For example, where large quantities of books are to be stored as efficiently as possible, with little concern about the aesthetics of the area, function will probably direct the decision toward some kind of steel shelving. Where a look of tradition or luxury is desired, appearance will enter into the decision more, so wood shelving is more apt to be the choice.

Many libraries are forced, however, to select the shelving that is their second choice, for budgetary reasons. High-quality wood shelving is much more expensive than steel, so librarians are frequently forced to purchase steel when, from the standpoint of appearance, they would prefer wood. The combination of steel shelving with wood end panels can be a compromise; however, wood end panels designed with a lot of special detail can be very expensive also.

Wood Shelving

Most of the manufacturers selling a line of library technical furniture make wood shelving. It is significant that these companies sell shelving designed specifically for library use. Many contract furniture companies and office supply houses sell products that are advertised as library shelving; however, when selecting shelving, the librarian must know exactly what type of construction is being provided. Since the specifications of the acceptable products are very similar, it is easy to check products from other manufacturers to see if they are comparable. Brodart, Buckstaff, Gaylord, Library Bureau, McDole, Texwood, Tuohy, and Worden, for example, all sell wood shelving of comparable quality.

Wood shelving constructed of particleboard shelves, end panels, and intermediate panels is not as satisfactory as that made with components of solid wood; particleboard shelves and upright panels are apt to sag or warp under the weight of books. Standard wood shelving that can be reliably used in the library has the following general specifications (See Figure 10):

End and intermediate panels. Panels, 1″ to 1¼″ thick, constructed of five-ply lumber core with a solid wood edge band, edge-glued wood panels, butcher block, or plank oak.

Top. Three-ply particleboard or five-ply lumber core with veneer facing or solid plank construction, ¾″ thick.

Base. Five-ply lumber core or solid edge-glued wood panels, ¾″ thick.

Shelves. Solid edge-glued wood panels with strips of wood less than 4″ wide, sometimes with a solid wood nosing, or five-ply lumber core, ¾″ thick.

Shelf support. Shelf pins placed at 1″ increments in holes in the upright panels, or flush-mounted aluminum shelf standards (K-V track) to hold clips for adjustment at ½″ increments.

Joinery. Metal-to-metal joining of panels to tops and bases with bushings, Rosans, or heliocoils used with bolts and washers.

Wood shelving is of the starter/adder type; that is, only the first section of each range (the starter) has two vertical panels, while subsequent sections (the adders) have only one panel. Back panels are available from all of the manufacturers, if they are desired. Wood shelves come in standard 8″, 10″, 12″, and 16″ sizes with bookstacks 42″, 60″, 82″, and 96″ high.

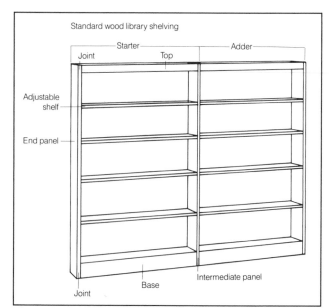

Figure 10. Standard wood library shelving.

Steel Shelving

For the last twenty years, there has been little stability in the steel shelving industry. Even though some manufacturers have produced shelving for many years, these companies have still undergone a variety of changes. Factories have been taken over by new owners or managers, the same product has been marketed under more than one name, and plants have closed, only to be opened again several years later.

For example, the Aetnastack plant closed in 1987; nevertheless, at the American Library Association Midwinter Meeting in January 1988, Aetnastack was exhibited by its new owner, Montel, a shelving company based in Canada. Montel had been making the carriage-and-track assembly for the movable system sold as the Aetnastack mobile product. Later in 1988, the Andrew Wilson Company declared bankruptcy and was subsequently purchased by Borroughs. At the same time, a new company in library shelving, MJ Industries, began selling bookstacks that are nearly identical to Wilson shelving. Products also change as new library materials require different kinds of storage or display units (e.g., compact discs), as better ways of manufacturing a product are developed, or as new trends are preferred by consumers for aesthetic reasons.

Because fluctuations in the industry are likely to continue, a librarian selecting steel shelving is best advised to consider the brands in the following discussion *only as a starting point.* Companies are going in and out of business so frequently that it is impossible to write about particular brands and expect them to be the same for years, or even months, to come. The specific products are discussed in order to illustrate which qualities in shelving are satisfactory or unsatisfactory. The information can then be used either to evaluate new lines of shelving or to re-evaluate older products.

There are only a few manufacturers of good-quality steel library shelving. The total market remains about the same size year after year, as new libraries replace older facilities, or as small additions are made to existing bookstacks. As in the case of other library technical furnishings, the major manufacturers of steel bookstacks exhibit at the American Library Association conventions and at state or regional conferences. Because these companies are primarily in the business of making bookstacks rather than other kinds of steel shelving, they are more apt to focus on serving the library market and, therefore, are more attuned to consumer demands.

There are many other steel shelving lines that are not specifically designed for libraries. These products are less likely to hold up when fully loaded with books, may not have easily interchangeable parts, and probably cannot store materials as effectively or as attractively as true library bookstacks.

The process of selecting library furnishings, as noted earlier, begins with deciding the function of the various items. Likewise, in the case of shelving, it is the responsibility of the librarian to decide what use will be made of the bookstacks, and the level of quality needed in each situation. As an example, it is obvious that a special library that stores mostly oversized, heavy volumes like law books may require different shelving than a small public library with a general collection. The attributes of various brands of shelving will be discussed here. The librarian using the information should understand that some situations may not require the most stable product nor the one with the best paint finish, etc.; however, it is assumed that everyone will want to get the highest quality for the money. The products with the best features may not be (and often are not) the ones that are the highest in price. Also, because the business is so unstable and competitive, the high-priced product today may be a bargain tomorrow. Furthermore, the price may depend on conditions of which the librarian is unaware, such as the lack of qualified installers in the area, the closing of a factory, or a manufacturer's overstock of a particular product.

While the discussion here describes steel shelving in some depth, there are other details, regarding anchoring in unusual situations and the use of bookstacks for seismic zones, for example, that are not included. These considerations can be discussed with vendors, other librarians, or, ideally, a consultant or engineer familiar with the particular problem.

The major manufacturers of steel library bookstacks over the past few years have been Aetnastack, Andrew Wilson, Estey, and Library Bureau. Other names in the business, now or in the recent past, are Spacemaster Systems (a division of the Reflector Hardware Corporation); Filing Equipment, Inc. (FEI); Interroyal; Republic Steel; and Ames. Catalog sales and bid purchases are also available from standard library suppliers like Gaylord, Brodart, and Highsmith. In the last several years, products manufactured in other countries have also been marketed in some areas of the United States. Notable among these are The Danish Library Design Bureau and an offshoot of this company, Library Steel Stacks. Library Steel Stacks provide essentially the same product as DLDB, but are manufactured in Mexico rather than in Denmark and are less expensive. Johl Library Systems, manufactured by All-Steel in Canada, and Montel have also recently exhibited at ALA. (Johl was sold to Spacesaver, a manufacturer of movable shelving, in 1988.)

Steel bookstacks consist of two upright, slotted columns that are connected at top and bottom by other channels of steel (spreaders). The frame (uprights and spreaders) either intermembers with a base bracket or rests on a leg base. Cantilevered shelves are then held by brackets that hang from slots in the uprights. The slots are spaced 1″ on center for the full height of the uprights, thereby allowing adjustment of the shelves in 1″ increments. The bookstacks may have a closed base or kick plate, canopy tops, end panels, and a number of accessories.

Double-faced (two-sided) sections of shelving are usually freestanding, while single-faced shelving must be anchored to a wall. In order to gain stability in the former's installation, the base of freestanding, double-faced shelving should be wider than the adjustable shelves placed above it. For example, with two 10″ adjustable shelves placed on either side of a double-faced section, a 24″ base shelf will be used, just as with 8″ adjustable shelves, a 20″ base shelf is appropriate. Shelves come in standard lengths of 30″ and 36″. Standard heights for steel bookstacks include 42″, 66″, 78″, 84″, and 90″. Adjustable shelves are standard in depths of 8″, 9″, 10″, and 12″; double-faced base shelves are 16″, 18″, 20″, and 24″. The depth dimensions of the adjustable shelves are "nominal," that is, they indicate the depth from the front edge of the shelf to the imaginary centerline of the shelving frame. For adjustable shelves, then, the *actual* depth of the shelf is 1″ less than the nominal.

Bookstacks designed specifically for libraries by the major manufacturers are constructed of the following gauges of steel:

Uprights: #14–#16 gauge
Spreaders: #14–#16 gauge
Shelves: #18–#19 gauge
Brackets: #16 gauge

Closed base: #18–#19 gauge
Open-base feet: #11–#14 gauge

Since there is nothing to prevent a manufacturer from changing the material used in shelving, it is best to purchase from a manufacturer of known reliability and verify the latest specifications, especially if a product has not been purchased by the library for several years.

There are several types of cantilevered steel shelving. Until the 1970s, most double-faced, freestanding library shelving was of the type that is stabilized longitudinally along the range by the addition of sway braces—diagonal steel rods tightened by means of a turnbuckle—placed every few sections. There is little doubt that sway braces, if properly installed, add to the stability of the shelving. However, there is a safety factor to be considered: because the sway braces are visible and easily accessible, it is possible for someone to tamper with them. While this may seem a remote possibility, it has happened. If a library staff member or patron does not realize the vital function of the rods and loosens one of the turnbuckles on the braces, the whole range of shelving can fall horizontally. Steel shelving can also be braced by adding strut channels or cross ties, which are placed perpendicularly to the range and tie one range to the next.

This type of shelving consists of starters and adders. That is, one section at the beginning of each range (the starter) includes both sides of the frame, with the second column acting as the upright for that section, as well as serving as one upright for the next section. Adder sections, then, have only one upright, so that once the starter is in place, all subsequent sections share one upright between them. With this type of shelving, starters and adders cannot be interchanged, and each range requires one starter.

Starter/adder shelving often has some kind of T- or footed-base in a variety of designs. Estey manufactures two kinds of starter/adder shelving, both of which require sway braces. The first has an open T-base. The upright is a one-piece column of steel. The base is inserted approximately five inches into the upright column. The more popular Estey starter/adder product is placed on a Z-shaped base that is designed for extra stability, and has a kick plate that gives the shelving a closed-base appearance.

Wilson's T-bar leg-base shelving has a welded frame, with the bottom spreader welded several inches up from the base of the uprights. The uprights are notched to fit around the T-bar leg base. Because a base is shared by adjoining sections, the shelving is starter/adder, but requires no sway braces. Aetnastack has a T-base product similar to Wilson's.

Unlike the other major manufacturers, Library Bureau considers starter/adder shelving its best-selling product. Adjoining sections share an upright that consists of two C-channels back-to-back with an additional piece of steel, called a web stiffener. These three components are welded together, providing a very strong upright. The shelving does require sway braces. The top spreader and base brackets are bolted to the uprights, and the system has a one-piece closed base. Library Bureau also makes a T-base shelving.

The Danish Library Design Bureau shelving is of starter/adder construction with a T-base of #11 gauge steel welded to the uprights. Spreaders attach to the uprights with a hook-in type assembly. The shelving can be open-based or, with the addition of base panels or kick plates, can become a closed-based system. No sway braces are used; however, the manufacturer recommends that three crossbars or spreaders be used on every fifth section of shelving 90″ high or taller. Library Steel Stacks have essentially the same design as the Danish line; however, the spreaders are attached to the uprights by allen screws that go into the uprights. On shelving 90″ or taller, the manufacturer recommends three spreaders on every third section.

The Johl and Montel shelving are starter/adder bookstacks with hook-in type spreaders. Uprights are welded to a T-base used either with or without kick plates. FEI's library shelving is another system with a hook-in or snap-together type of assembly. The shelving consists of uprights that serve as legs, single-sided base shelf brackets, a top spreader, base and adjustable shelves, kickplates, and two hook-in type steel spreaders (referred to in the company's literature as steel sway braces) in each three-foot section. Spacemaster's steel shelving is a T-base system with seamless uprights and two "Z" shaped hook-in type spreaders in each section. Either open- or closed-base designs are available.

During the 1960s and 1970s, the major shelving manufacturers began making bookstacks of one-piece welded-frame construction. They continue, however, to produce starter/adder shelving. The bookstacks of the older design are often sold as additional pieces for existing installations. One major manufacturer now claims that 80 percent of the company's shelving business is welded frame, while another reports that 80 percent of its product sales is of the sway-brace design.

Aetnastack, Estey, Gaylord, Library Bureau, Andrew Wilson, and now MJ Industries, all sell a welded-frame bookstack. As the name implies, welded-frame shelving consists of uprights and spreaders that are welded together, so that each section includes a four-sided frame. In their descriptive literature, all of the manufacturers of welded frames emphasize the strength provided by the welding of the uprights to the spreaders. There is more flexibility in the use of a welded-frame system, because there is no need for a starter section in each range: any frame is interchangeable with any other frame. Each frame is shipped as one module, so the shelving is easier to install than bookstacks that require bolting the upright to the spreader. Because sway braces are not necessary, the shelving has a cleaner appearance, and there is nothing to prevent shelving of oversized volumes that may extend beyond the back edge of the shelf. (See Figure 11).

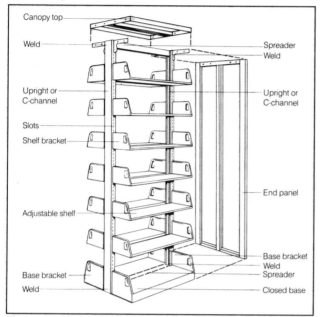

Figure 11. Steel library shelving, one double-faced section of a welded-frame system.

Under ordinary conditions (level floors, no special requirements for seismic zones, etc.), welded-frame shelving should not require any special bracing. A consumer would be wise to investigate carefully if a vendor claims to sell a stable, welded-frame product, but then refers the customer to several projects where cross-ties or sway braces have been added to the shelving following the initial installation.

There are some subtle differences among the frames of the various manufacturers. Estey, for example, has twice as many right-angle bends in its uprights as any other product (sixteen in a double-faced section, rather than eight). Also, there are small differences in the size of the uprights from product to product. Estey's upright measures 1¼″ at the front and rear and 2½″ on the sides, with a ¾″ stiffening flange. Wilson and Gaylord have an upright that is 1¼″ × 2″, with a ½″ stiffening flange. Aetnastack has a 1⁵⁄₁₆″ × 2″ upright, with a ½″ stiffening flange; while Library Bureau has a 1³⁄₁₆″ × 2″ upright, with a ½″ stiffening flange.

On Estey, Wilson, and Gaylord, the closed side of the C-channel of the upright is bolted to the closed side of the adjoining upright. This design allows the spreader to fit inside and to be welded into the C-channel. (See Figure 12). Library Bureau likewise welds the frame with the closed sides of the C-channel bolted together, but the spreader is welded over the top of the upright, and a web stiffener is bolted between adjoining uprights for extra strength. Unlike the manufacturers mentioned above, Aetnastack bolts the adjoining uprights together with the open side of the C-channels together. The spreader is welded to the flat side of the upright. While Aetnastack gains a more finished appearance with this design, the other manufacturers claim that bolting the C-channels back-to-back results in a stronger upright.

Figure 12. Detail of a welded steel shelving frame showing the C-channel on an upright. The C-channel on this upright measures 2″ on the long side of the C and 1¼″ on the two short sides of the C. Two ½″ stiffening flanges are welded to the spreader. *Photograph courtesy of Gaylord Bros., Syracuse, N.Y.*

In terms of performance for most libraries, it is doubtful that the extra bends or the extra parts of an inch of steel need to be determining factors in deciding which type of welded-frame shelving to select. While it is important to have a product that holds together and does not bend or break with use, the stability of the bookstacks should be the primary consideration in selection.

An important element in the stability of the welded-frame shelving is the construction of the base bracket. Estey, Wilson, and Gaylord all have a one-piece base bracket that fits tightly around the welded-frame upright and has a 90-degree flange at the bottom that rests on the floor. The base bracket of one section is bolted to the bracket on the adjoining section and can telescope up or down the upright to allow for leveling the shelving. (See Figure 13). Library Bureau has a one-piece base bracket, but it does not fit around the upright. Rather, it has a one-piece base bracket that fits between the two uprights below the web stiffener. The base bracket is then bolted to the uprights.

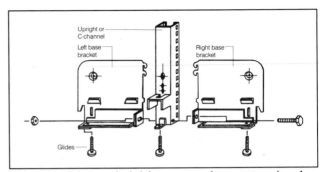

Figure 14. Other steel shelving systems have a two-piece base bracket that bolts to either side of the upright. *Drawing courtesy of Montel/Aetnastack.*

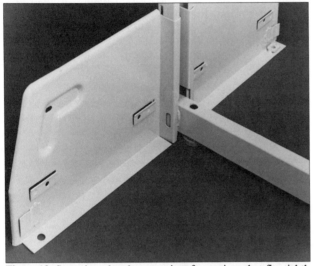

Figure 13. Some base brackets consist of one piece that fits tightly around the welded-frame upright. The bracket has a 90-degree flange at the bottom that rests on the floor. *Photograph courtesy of Gaylord Bros., Syracuse, N.Y.*

On each double-faced section, Aetnastack has a two-piece base bracket that is bolted to either side of the upright. (See Figure 14). Likewise, there is a separate base shelf on either side of the double-faced section, with the bottom spreader filling the space between the two base shelves. While the one-piece, wrap-around base bracket (of Estey, MJ, Gaylord) maximizes the stability available in a welded-frame bookstack, the two-piece design of Aetnastack has the advantage of allowing the user to convert the shelving from double- to single-faced: one-half of the assembly from a double-faced section (one bracket and one base shelf) can be used for a single-faced section and, conversely, the base assembly from two single-faced sections can be placed back-to-back to convert them to one double-faced section.

According to the trusted source, *Planning Academic and Research Library Buildings* by Keyes Metcalf, canopy tops, steel end panels, and one-piece bases all contribute to the stability of steel bookstacks. Another major factor in stability is the capability that the user will have for leveling the shelving. Obviously, all of the features that make the shelving stable as a unit are of little value if the stacks are listing one way or another on an uneven floor. Most shelving is leveled by adjusting built-in

threaded levelers. This method has proven to be reliable. Wilson, Gaylord, Aetnastack, and Estey provide two adjustable levelers on each frame. Estey and Aetnastack go one step further, however, by providing levelers on the base brackets on both sides of a double-faced section. The Danish Library Design Bureau and Library Steel Stacks products have levelers mounted 1″ from the outer edge of the feet. Library Bureau shelving is leveled by shimming— that is, slipping a thin piece of wood or metal under the base to compensate for uneven places in the floor.

Two kinds of paint are used for finishing steel shelving. Most companies use a process in which wet paint is electrostatically applied to the steel. Estey, The Danish Library Design Bureau, Library Steel Stacks, and MJ, however, use a dry powder paint that is applied electrostatically. With both wet and dry paint, the final step in the finishing process is baking the enamel. Proponents of the dry process claim that shelving with the powder paint has a better overall appearance; the shelving is more evenly coated because of the way the paint is applied. The powder paint provides a thicker coat of enamel, so when a shelf is nicked or bent, there is less chance of the finish chipping. Wet-process paint can, however, be touched up more successfully than dry-process products.

In addition to flat shelves for books, all of the manufacturers make a variety of specialty shelves and accessories that can be placed in standard frames. These include divider shelves with backs for picture books, plays, or pamphlets; hinged and fixed periodical display shelves; sliding or stationary reference shelves; phonograph record shelves; newspaper racks; storage lockers; and in-stack carrels. Many of the manufacturers sell shelves with adjustable backstops. A variation of this is the integral back shelf, where the back and shelf are both made of one piece of steel. The Danish Library Design Bureau, for example, sells a shelf with a bent-up backstop of 2″. (See Figure 15). Wilson and Gaylord also make an integral back shelf. All of the backstops can be used as a rail to hold a wire book support which moves across the length of the shelf on a nylon runner. Other available book supports include wire supports that attach to the underside of the shelf, supports that hook on the front of the shelf, and "findable" book supports. Gaylord makes an excellent book support of heavy-gauge steel.

Figure 15. The integral back shelf has a back and shelf made of one piece of steel. *Photograph courtesy of The Danish Library Design Bureau.*

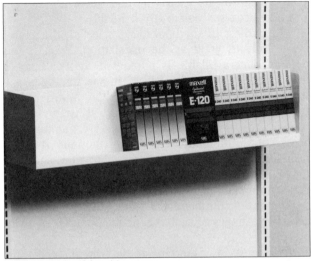

Figure 16A. Shelf for video tapes.

Several of the shelving companies have responded to the public librarian's interest in merchandising of library materials. Display stacks usually include slanted shelves that allow for the attractive shelving of books face out. Most of the companies will make lighted shelves when they are specified by the purchaser.

No American company, however, has begun to compete with The Danish Library Design Bureau or the related product, Library Steel Stacks, in addressing the possibilities of effective display of library materials. In addition to having lighted shelves and signage as standard products, these companies also have a number of useful and attractive accessories that fit onto their shelving. They sell, for example, a metal browsing box with adjustable dividers that can be used for paperbacks, picture books, and records; acrylic cassette holders; a slanted, two-tiered cassette shelf, on which cassettes can be effectively displayed face out; a slanted shelf that can be used for paperbacks, talking books, or compact discs; a record hanger; a folding shelf that is mounted on the end of the range; and a fixed steel display shelf mounted on the end panel. (See Figures 16A–C).

Steel shelving can be used with steel or wood end panels or with end panels faced with high-pressure laminate. Shelving 42″ high can be more effectively used as a display or worksurface if it has a laminate top. In public areas, 90″-high shelving is often used without canopy tops. This is, of course, an economical choice; furthermore, it is easier to see the contents of the shelves when light from the

Figure 16B. Browsing box for compact discs, records, or paperbacks.

Figure 16C. Double-tiered shelf for audio cassettes.

ceiling is not blocked by the shelving tops. Shelving shorter than 90″ is often used with canopy tops in order to give the shelving a more finished appearance. Backs for steel shelving and fillers for corners and odd-sized spaces are also available.

Regardless of the bookstacks selected, the shelving is only as good as the installation. Even if the best product available is purchased, it won't serve the intended purpose safely if it has not been installed so as to be stable. Once the librarian has supplied a layout for the shelving, it is up to the supplier to see that the bookstacks are put together according to the manufacturer's instructions. It is the installer's responsibility to see that the shelving range is placed in a straight line and leveled for maximum stability. In unusual situations, the installer may recommend the installation of cross ties across the ranges of shelving, or the addition of sway braces.

While it is important to let the installers do their job, it is a good idea to see how a couple of sections are put together. Installation is often subcontracted to another company by the supplier, so it is possible that the subcontractor will try to cut corners on hardware and labor. Reliable manufacturers and salespeople want the job to be properly installed.

Once the installation is complete, check the shelving for stability. When the shelves are shaken, there should be very little movement either horizontally along the range, or laterally from side to side. Wall shelving should be anchored securely to the wall. The installer should have touched up nicks and scratches in the paint; these are the natural result of shipping and installing the shelving. Bent or badly marred shelves, end panels, and tops should be replaced by the supplier. Manufacturers know that there will almost always be some small amount of damage in shipping.

If the shelving is not stable, the librarian should not give in to the argument that once shelves are fully loaded, the stacks won't sway. When shelving has been filled with books, any instability becomes a real danger. Check the shelving again when there *are* books on it, and insist that it be leveled properly.

The industry standard is a one-year warranty on steel shelving. Library Bureau has a standard five-year warranty on its products. Other manufacturers may provide a warranty of longer than one year, if it is requested. The manufacturer and vendor have a responsibility to live up to their warranties on parts and labor. Once a job has been accepted as satisfactory, however, it is unreasonable to expect a supplier or installer to come back, free of charge, to correct a situation that is the result of something in the building, such as uneven floors or walls, and not a problem with the product or installation.

Over the years, shelving that was once properly installed may become unstable, as bolts loosen or the building settles. Go back and check older installations occasionally. If the shelving is now unstable, ask a local vendor for the name of a qualified installer who can be hired to do whatever is necessary to improve the stability of the bookstacks. Occasionally a librarian will inherit older shelving that was not installed properly initially. The fact that none of the shelving has fallen in several years (luckily!) should not deter a responsible person from going to the expense of having the situation corrected immediately.

Wood/Steel Systems

Another choice in shelving is to combine wood and steel. The standard way to accomplish this is to order a steel shelving system and have wood end panels manufactured by one of the furniture companies placed on the end sections of the ranges. Another kind of bookstack system, however, consists of steel shelves used with wood uprights; these are starter/adder systems. Brodart's Omega shelving and Library Bureau's Pioneer system, for example, are essentially their solid wood cases used with steel, instead of wood, shelves. Aetnastack, Brodart, Gaylord, and Library Bureau are some of the companies that sell *display* units with steel shelves and wood-veneered end panels. These units are designed for shelving materials face out on shelves that tip up at an angle. The display shelving is often available with signage and/or lights.

Highsmith sells a Scandinavian-made system, Scania Wood-With-Steel, that consists of upright panels used with steel shelves. (See Figure 17). The panels are constructed of particleboard core, faced with beechwood veneer, and have a solid beechwood radius edge 1″ thick. The system can have an open base, or a wood kickplate can be added for a closed-base look. The unit is stabilized by a 16-gauge welded-steel frame that is placed in each three-foot section. The frame is not the same height as the shelving on a regular welded-steel shelving; rather, it is 34″ square, regardless of the height of the shelving. The frame is bolted through one frame, the intermediate upright, and into the frame on the next section. Like the Danish product discussed earlier, the Scania Wood-With-Steel shelving has a number of interesting display units, including a single-faced, zigzag arrangement; acrylic magazine and literature display units; and a wire paperback carousel that fits on the end panel. The units can be purchased with light fixtures.

Figure 17. Scania Wood-With-Steel shelving can be assembled in a zigzag arrangement. *Photograph courtesy of Highsmith.*

Compact Movable Shelving

Background information about the kinds of compact storage available can be found in "Movable Compact Shelving: A Survey of U.S. Suppliers and Library Users" by Herbert Hannah and Nancy Knight in *Library Technology Reports* and in *Planning Academic and Research Library Buildings.* Keep in mind that many of the products discussed in the *LTR* article have changed. The following discussion will be limited to systems that are essentially mobile ranges of shelving (similar to traditional stationary units) that make more efficient use of space by eliminating the need for most aisle space.

An article by Charles Smith on compact movable shelving in the June 1987 issue of *Library Administration and Management* discusses the results of a survey conducted by the LAMA/BES Equipment Committee. It is interesting to note that, of the eight companies that supply compact shelving listed there, at least one is no longer in business with the brand name given (Elecompack). On the other hand, several companies that are relatively prominent in the business at this writing are not included (such as TAB Products, Kardex, Acme Visible). The list does, however, include several manufacturers who have been involved with movable shelving for several years (Aetnastack, Library Bureau, Lundia, RHC-Spacemaster, Spacesaver, and White Office Systems). The article thus illustrates that the compact shelving business is as unstable as the steel shelving industry. It is quite likely that during the time it has taken for this information to be published, the industry will have changed again and new companies will be selling compact systems. While there are very few manufacturers of steel library shelving, there are many vendors selling movable shelving products.

There are essentially two components to a movable-shelving system: the carriage, with some kind of wheel that runs on a metal track, and the shelving, which rests on the carriage. The manufacturing is very complicated. Some companies, like Library Bureau, sell a system that includes their own steel shelving product, but which is placed on a carriage manufactured by another company. At the present, Library Bureau's compact system uses an RHC-Spacemaster carriage. At one time, the carriage and track were supplied by Montel, the Canadian company that bought out part of Aetnastack when that company went bankrupt in 1987. The Aetnastack compact system is based on the Montel product. To complicate the industry even further, some companies supply carriages sold under another brand name, but sell the same product under their own manufacturing name as well. Some companies manufacture all of the product except for the shelving that goes on it. These companies, for example, may use Library Bureau or Estey shelving for a library situation. Another possibility is that the company manufactures both the carriage and the shelving; Lundia is an example of this kind of product. The point of all this for the consumer is to indicate the absolute necessity to research the product carefully before purchasing a movable system. A company may do something as simple as placing standard shelving on wheels and then claim that this is a movable system, but with several satisfactory, well-tested products on the market, there is no need to consider a jerry-built system. It is also very important when developing specifications to consider the details of the construction and materials of the product. Most manufacturers sell several different grades of movable shelving. Some vendors have been known to say they can meet specifications, because they do make a top-of-the-line product that can match the specs. Unfortunately, however, when they bid, they substitute their less-expensive product for the better one. If the unsuspecting consumer does not go over the details of the bid very carefully, and assumes that the product will meet specifications, s/he may find out too late that the level of quality desired was not received.

The advertising literature of the various companies is sometimes confusing. It is very difficult to look at three or four company brochures and find very much to compare. One company, for example, discusses the details of twelve complicated systems in its short specification booklet. Many companies, on the other hand, explain very little in their advertising brochures. Since you can't rely on the literature, remember to work with a reliable vendor, check with previous users, and, above all, know the right questions to ask. (See page 35 for a list of appropriate questions.)

Because of the frequent changes made in shelving and the variety of products available, information about specific brands of movable shelving may not be useful for very long. For that reason, the discussion that follows will cover the components of movable compact systems, and the details of material and construction that should be considered when selecting a particular product to specify.

Compact movable shelving was once used mainly in academic and special libraries where access was limited to staff or special users. This is no longer the case. Many public libraries are now adding compact systems to older buildings, and installing it in new buildings, in order to make the best use of limited space.

Function and maintenance are obviously the prime considerations when selecting compact movable shelving. While appearance may be considered in some situations, it definitely should not be the determining factor in selecting which brand to purchase. Important considerations when selecting a compact movable system include the following:

1. Who will be the major users of the shelving? Will they be able to operate the system easily and efficiently?

2. How often will the system need to be accessed, and by how many users at one time?
3. What kinds of materials will be stored in the shelving? Is this the most efficient way of storing these items?
4. Will service be readily available if repairs are needed on the system?
5. In a new building, is movable shelving included to save space less expensive than adding more square feet to the size of the facility?
6. High-density storage requires a floor or foundation that can hold more weight per square foot than standard shelving. In an older building, has an engineer verified the load-bearing capability of the floor? In a new building, is the greater cost of building the area to carry the additional weight of compact shelving justified? Would it be less expensive to add more square feet of space to the building and include more standard shelving? (Recommendations regarding the load-bearing capability of floors beneath compact systems range all the way from 200 to 450 lbs. per square foot, depending on the materials to be stored. For this reason, always get the opinion of a reliable engineer before purchasing compact shelving.)

There are three kinds of movable systems: strictly manual compact shelving, which is moved when the user pulls or pushes the ranges along a track; mechanically assisted manual systems, which use some kind of crank to operate a chain, gear, and sprocket system to turn a drive shaft; and electrically

Figure 18. Compact movable-shelving systems are used in all kinds of libraries, and are located in public, as well as closed-stack areas. *Photograph courtesy of Spacesaver Corporation.*

operated systems. Both cantilevered and four-post or post-lock types of shelving are used on the movable systems. In addition, a wide variety of other storage units can be placed on the carriages for use in museums, hospitals, banks, or data processing departments.

Different brands of compact movable shelving vary according to the load-bearing capabilities of their carriages, the maximum length of a range that can be moved satisfactorily, and the number of tracks needed for each range. For this reason, it is necessary to decide what size system is needed by the library, and then to talk to reliable suppliers about the specific manner in which the system can be designed to fit into the space available.

Manual systems are used in areas needing a limited amount of high-density storage that does not need to be accessed frequently. The ranges are usually no more than 6 feet long. Even with this limit on the range length to restrict the weight to be moved, some people would have difficulty moving the shelving. Because the ranges are moved strictly by hand, there is also a limit to the number of ranges that can be used efficiently.

Mechanically assisted and electrically operated compact systems can include more long ranges than the manual shelving, but can still be moved easily. The decision regarding which of the three kinds of movable shelving to select may be based to some extent on the funds available for the project. Electrically operated compact shelving is more expensive than either of the manual systems. On the other hand, the electrical systems have better safety systems, can include built-in lighting, provide faster access, and can be operated with less physical effort. Also, the systems can be designed so that the material stored there can be accessed by computer.

It is possible to place standard steel shelving already owned by the library on movable carriages. This should only be done, however, if the shelving is a high-quality product that is strong and stable in spite of previous use. Get the advice of a reliable vendor. If the vendor says the existing shelving is not suitable for use on a carriage, take her/his advice seriously; if necessary, get a second opinion. The preceding information about quality in steel shelving can also be used by librarians in forming opinions in this regard.

Many of the problems to be overcome in designing a satisfactory movable shelving system can be understood with an elementary knowledge of the physical forces involved in moving several fully loaded ranges of library shelving. Force, of course, is needed to overcome inertia and get the shelving moving and—more important from the standpoint of safety and stability—also to stop it. The more that is stored on the shelving, the greater the effect of momentum once the shelving is moving, and the

greater will be the force needed to stop the movable range from slamming into a stationary range and rebounding in the opposite direction.

In terms of use, then, once the shelving is moving, there can be a problem stopping a range gently enough to keep it from bouncing back against a person or object between the ranges. The shelving should be designed to minimize wear on the system caused by the constant heavy jolts when the ranges start or stop. From a safety standpoint, there must be some means of preventing someone from closing an aisle already in use, and some way of ensuring absolutely that the range will not tip over. The track must be level and designed in such a manner that the wheels of the carriage do not "jump the track." On long ranges, problems can also develop with the drive shaft that moves the shelving, if the shaft is not designed with the tolerance necessary to withstand the twisting motion that occurs as several sections of shelving are moved along by wheels on several different tracks.

Starting from the floor, consider the various elements that make up the compact movable shelving system. (See Figure 19). The rails or track can be used in either new or old buildings. Ideally, the system will be part of the building program, designed along with the facility. Most systems allow for recessing the track in the floor, so that the rails are flush with the finished floor. (See Figure 20). This allows for easier use with book trucks and safer entry by the staff. The architect should work directly with the shelving supplier, so that the building is designed to accommodate the movable system with regard to the track, the load-bearing capabilities of the floor, and the availability of adequate power for electrical systems.

In older buildings, the system must be placed on a plywood deck that may be anywhere from ¾″ to 1½″ above the floor. Some systems are always installed on a deck. The disadvantage of having to add a deck, of course, is that ramping is necessary to enter the aisle. The deck is also an additional expense.

In order to have the shelving run smoothly and correctly, the track must be level. Some systems use shims at regular intervals—every 10″ to 12″—under the track in order to level it. The advantage to this method is that the shims can be easily adjusted as the floor changes, without having to remove the deck. Other systems level the track by placing the rails on a surface of grout or quick-dry cement, which is added to the floor. This method can cause problems if the grout breaks down and crumbles along the edges of the system, or even under the track. The process of leveling as the floor shifts in the future may also be more complicated, if the decking has to be removed for releveling. In addition, the grout must be removed in order to restore

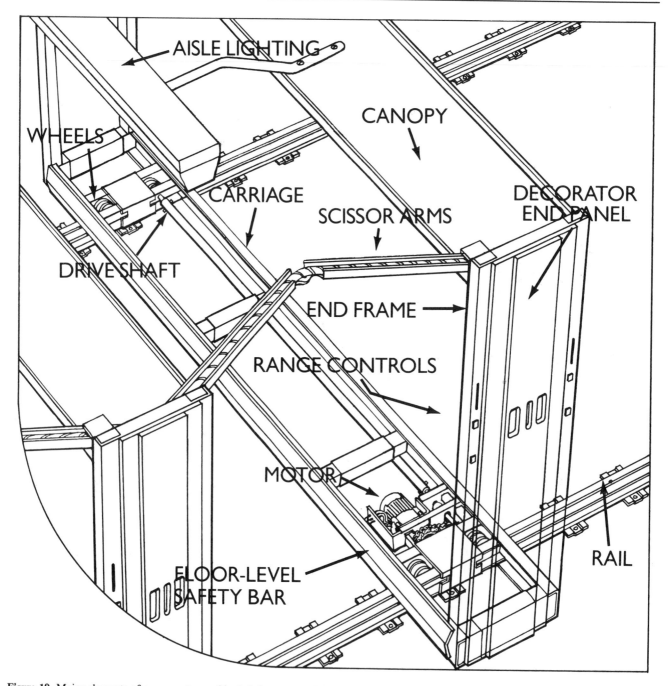

Figure 19. Major elements of a compact movable-shelving system. *Drawing courtesy of Kardex Systems.*

the floor, if the system is moved. Some systems installed on a deck have built-in levelers that allow for leveling the track without removing the deck.

The wheels of the movable systems range in size from 2¾″ to 5″ in diameter. Heavy-duty systems have steel wheels, which are from 4½″ to 5″ in diameter. The wheels must be designed so that they will stay on the track. Most of the systems have a double-flanged wheel; others have a wheel with a center flange that fits into a groove in the track. (See Figure 21). On the better systems, there is a double flange on every wheel in the system, and every wheel

helps to drive the system. On other systems, only some wheels are flanged and help to drive and guide the shelving; the other wheels are there just to support the carriage. These other wheels do not help to keep the system on track, but are dragged along by the drive wheels, without helping to move the shelves. All wheels should be permanently lubricated and sealed.

The wheels are mounted on a drive shaft made of either tubular or solid steel. (See Figure 22). The proponents of the tubular shaft claim that the solid steel is more apt to break from the torsional move-

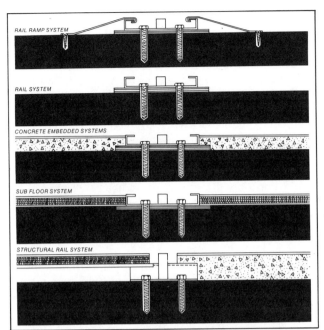

Figure 20. The track for movable shelving can be recessed in the concrete slab of a new building, or added to the floor of an existing building. *Drawing courtesy of Kardex Systems.*

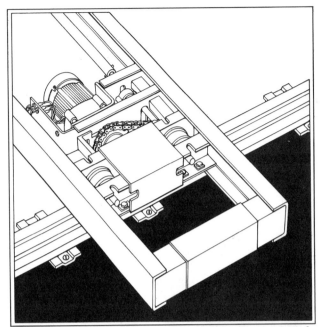

Figure 22. The carriage of a movable system serves as a base for the shelving; houses the motor, drive shaft, and wheels; and accommodates safety bars and limit switches. *Drawing courtesy of Kardex Systems.*

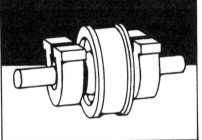

DOUBLE FLANGED
WHEELS WITH PILLOW BLOCKS

Figure 21. Many movable-shelving systems have double-flanged wheels that ride on the track. *Drawing courtesy of Kardex Systems.*

ment of the system, but that the tubular shaft is more flexible and, therefore, has a greater tolerance for twisting motions. The high-quality systems all have a continuous drive shaft that runs the full length of each range of shelving. The carriage of the movable system acts as the base for the shelving. There is some disagreement among the manufacturers as to the best material for the carriage. Most of the systems have welded-steel frames; the manufacturers claim the steel is needed for strength. The most reliable steel systems have welded rather than bolted frames. Spacesaver, however, has an aluminum frame that the company claims is strong enough to carry the system and has the advantage of being of a lighter weight.

The frame of the Kardex system has a unique feature that adds to the strength of the product.

While the end frames of all of the systems serve to hold the end panel of the stacks and the shelving controls, the Kardex end frame is a welded-steel structural element that intermembers with the base of the carriage and adds to the stability of the shelving by limiting rocking and flexing as the ranges move along the track. (See Figure 23).

On the mechanical-assist systems, the gear-and-sprocket assembly is essentially the same from system to system. (See Figure 24). Likewise, all are operated by turning some kind of crank or wheel located on the end panel of the ranges of shelving. Several ranges can be moved by cranking the system at one location.

The well-known, electrically operated systems have a motor on each carriage that turns the drive shaft for that range. The motors should have automatic thermal-overload protection. In the earlier discussion about electrical systems in furniture, a distinction was made between those products that contain UL-recognized components and those that have their entire electrical system UL-listed. A similar situation exists with compact movable shelving. While all of the systems include components that are UL-recognized, only some of them, such as Spacesaver's top-of-the-line model, Kardex, and TAB, have their complete electrical compact system UL-listed. This distinction can be important in writing specifications and setting the level of quality desired. Another electrical consideration is how the system will be powered. Some systems require a receptacle at the end of each range into which the cord for that one carriage is plugged. This means

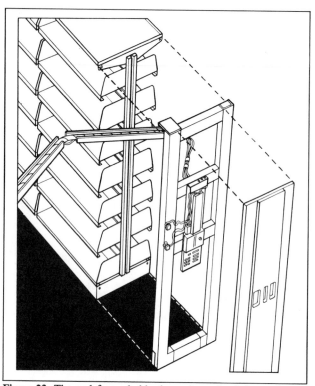

Figure 23. The end frame holds the end panels of the stacks and the shelving controls. The welded-steel end frame on the Kardex Kompakt system adds to the stability of the shelving. *Drawing courtesy of Kardex Systems.*

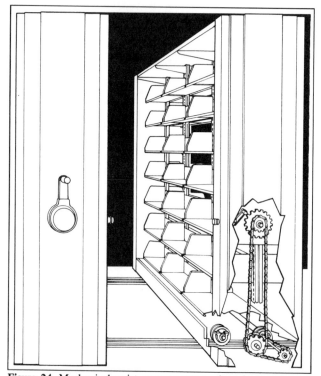

Figure 24. Mechanical-assist systems move when the user turns a handle that operates a gear-and-sprocket assembly. *Drawing courtesy of Kardex Systems.*

that as the shelving moves, the cords from each range are dragged back and forth. In the better systems, the entire unit (up to a maximum size) can be plugged into one power source. In the event of power failure, it is best to have a system equipped with mechanical override, so that the shelving can still be operated.

A mechanical-assist system should have some kind of safety feature that locks the aisle in use. Several of the systems have a locking device on the end panel. On the White system, for example, a safety knob on the end panel must be depressed by the user entering the aisle. The carriage cannot be moved until the knob is pulled out. Other systems employ a pin that is engaged in some fashion in order to lock the range in use.

The safety systems on electrical compact shelving are extremely important. While there was a time when the safety features of the manufacturers varied greatly, most of the well-known companies can now offer similar safety systems, at least as an option. There should be both a primary and a secondary system to protect users, and to prevent the aisle from closing on other objects, such as books, stools, etc. The primary system should be one that is activated in some way when the user opens an aisle and prepares to enter. In some systems, this may mean pressing an "open" button on the end of the range, which activates the secondary safety systems. Access to the aisle in another system is gained by a wave of the hand over the sensor control at the end of the range. In the less sophisticated and, certainly, less convenient systems, aisle access may be limited by such things as a rope that must be moved from one side of the aisle to the other in order to allow entry, or by warning lights or sounds indicating aisle use. Another system uses a safety "eye" that activates the safety system when someone enters the aisle. When a user leaves an aisle, the primary safety system on most movable shelving is reset either automatically or by the depression of a safety switch.

The secondary safety systems are fairly standard: a toe-level bar running the full length of the range, which stops the system when hit by a person or an object, and a waist-level bar that will likewise stop the system when hit. Be wary of safety devices that are attached by no more than double-stick tape and can easily fall off. All of the manufacturers offer some kind of safety floor, at least as an option. The floor prevents an aisle from closing if there is as little as 15 to 25 lbs. of pressure on it. While some customers insist on the floor, it is not necessary if the other safety systems mentioned above are well-designed and included in the shelving system.

Another useful feature that is available on some systems is a safety bypass that allows the operator to bypass the safety systems in a range in the case of a malfunction in that one range, without shutting the entire system off. On the Kardex system, for example, a bypass key is inserted into the range that is affected, and a chime sounds as a reminder that the safety system is not activated when that range is operated.

Another safety consideration in compact movable shelving is the availability of anti-tip devices on the system. Ideally, the system should have two kinds of anti-tip protection: an overhead system such as the scissor arms between the ranges on the TAB system, and anti-tip devices built into the track and carriage. Because of the problem of one range slamming into another, the system should also have some kind of limit switch or braking system that softens stopping.

There are some other features that can make a compact system more convenient; these are offered as options on some systems, but may be standard on others. As an example, overhead lighting, available on several systems, including Kardex and Spacesaver, is turned on when the button is pressed to activate the safety system for the aisle to be entered. The Acme Visible Magic Aisle system, among others, allows for multiple-aisle access in systems that will be used frequently. Other features available on some systems are the capability for temporarily converting a movable range into a stationary range, and the capability for restricting access to any number of ranges while permitting access to others. Most of the compact movable shelving can be locked to prevent access to the system.

While the carriage-and-track assembly is vital to the movable system, the quality of shelving desired should be clearly specified. The shelving that goes on the movable system should be the same high quality as that selected for use in the rest of the library. If the company selected makes its own shelving, use the same selection considerations with regard to construction and materials as were discussed previously. There may be some advantage to the library in terms of cost and flexibility of use if the compact system and regular shelving are the same brand.

A one-year warranty is fairly standard for compact movable shelving. The installers of the shelving should be factory-trained. The systems should be easily expandable and should allow for dismantling and moving to a new location. If an electrically operated system is to be used in an area where service is not readily available, it is important to select a system with controls that can be easily accessed and that has some self-diagnostic capabilities.

In summary, there are many questions to be considered when selecting a compact movable system. The following can be used as a guide in working with a vendor:

1. Can the rails be recessed, or will there be some kind of deck for the system? If there is a subfloor or deck, how high will it be?
2. How will the rail or track system be leveled?
3. How are the wheels designed and how do they fit into the track to prevent misalignment on the rails?
4. How is the carriage designed for strength? Is the end frame designed to contribute to the strength of the structure?
5. Is there a full-length drive shaft? How is it constructed? Are all wheels drive wheels?
6. What safety systems are available on the system? Are they convenient for the user? Are there both primary and secondary systems on an electrical system?
7. If the system is electrically operated, is the entire system UL-listed? Can the system be plugged into a single power source?
8. Does the electrical system have a mechanical override?
9. Does the system have both overhead and carriage-level anti-tip devices? Does the system have limit switches or a braking system?
10. What kind of shelving can be used on the system? Does it meet the criteria for strength and stability needed in any library shelving?
11. Does the system have features like multiple-aisle access, safety bypass of individual ranges, lighting, locks, and the capability for temporarily making a moving range stationary?
12. What is the warranty on the system?
13. Who will install and service the system?
14. Can the system be expanded or moved?

In closing, it must be reiterated that the specific shelving products discussed here may no longer be manufactured by next year or even next month. Products with the same or similar features to those discussed will be available, however, and the specifications can be compared with regard to construction and materials to the brands included in this chapter.

Chapter 5
Service Desks

Two stereotypical assumptions about librarians continue to be prevalent in spite of the efforts of library professionals to dispel them. First is the assumption that everyone who works in the library is a "librarian," and the second is that everyone who is a librarian loves to read and spends time reading on the job. Contrary to this distorted view of the profession, library work requires staff with a wide variety of expertise, experience, academic credentials, and knowledge. And, although many librarians love to read, most of the active members of the profession do well to find time to read off the job, much less during work time.

The active, varied nature of library work is evident in the planning of service desks, those areas in the library with the most staff/user interactions. While desks are designed on the basis of the functions to be performed there, there is a subjective element to the planning that is based on the philosophy of the librarian or the goals of the library. Librarians with several years of experience usually have considered or observed what they think makes a satisfactory reference or circulation desk.

There is probably no ideal service desk. What works in one location may not necessarily work in another; there are just too many variables to consider. With this in mind, the following chapter will review some of the many possibilities available for planning attractive, functional service locations in the library. For an excellent example of the problem-solving approach to planning a desk, see "Designing a Reference Desk" by Hugh Macdonald in the Fall 1986 *Texas Library Journal*. The article outlines the manner in which Texas Christian University Library went about defining its requirements for a desk and then specifying a design that would fulfill its needs.

Circulation and reference (or information) desks can be part of a building contract and, therefore, part of the millwork or cabinetry designed by the architect. Or they can be part of the furnishings purchased for a building. While "built-in" desks can work satisfactorily, there are some advantages to selecting units manufactured by a library furniture company. The latter are more likely to be modular in construction,

that is, built of standard modules that can be disassembled and relocated if major changes in the building are needed in the future. The desks are likely to be constructed of an outer "shell" that can be seen from the patrons' side. Standard modules are then placed into this shell on the working side of the desk. The modules are designed to include specific interior elements (shelves, file drawers, knee space, etc.) that will allow the staff to accomplish certain transactions effectively. If the desk is of modular construction, it can be reconfigured, or the interior changed, as transactions change over time. Another reason for purchasing the desk as a piece of furniture is that the better library and contract furniture manufacturers have addressed the need for effective power distribution and wire management. The library can take advantage of this experience and expertise by purchasing desks that have electrical systems designed into them. Both circulation and reference desks must be planned to accommodate a variety of kinds of electrical equipment. For this reason, one of the primary considerations in selecting a manufacturer for these items is the electrical system that can be provided. The information and criteria presented in Chapter 3 concerning electrical systems in library furnishings should be applied to the selection of desks to be purchased.

The purchase of a desk outside the building contract does not need to be a problem, if the desk is designed right along with the rest of the building. The general plans are determined in discussions with the architect early in the preliminary design phase of the building project. As planning continues, the architect is informed of the power requirements for the desk and given additional details about the desk as the design is refined. Finally, the supplier of the desk is required to make field measurements while the library is under construction. The vendor then passes on to the factory any required adjustments to ensure that the desk can be assembled correctly on the site.

Flexibility of design is essential in planning a desk. The circulation desk should be designed so that it can accommodate different kinds of equipment and varying functions in the future. It is usu-

Figure 25. The shape of a circulation desk can delineate work stations and establish the beginning of a queue for users. This desk was custom-designed by the author for Montrose Branch, Houston Public Library. It was made by Gayeski Furniture Coordinates and includes a Worden electrical system. *Photo: David J. Lund.*

ally a basic rectangle that allows for the flexibility of performing a number of functions within the same relatively small space. Angles in the desk, or zigzag and stairstep configurations of the modules add some interest to the shape of the desk, delineate work stations, and establish the beginning of a queue for users. In a library with a very small staff, the shape of the desk and its placement in a particular location may be determined by the fact that this is the only control point in the building. The desk may serve as the reference as well as the circulation desk.

The worksurface has to be long enough to accommodate the maximum number of staff members who may need to be assigned there, and deep enough to hold the equipment to be used on it. At the same time, it must not be so wide that staff members cannot comfortably pass books across to the user. The desk height will be determined by the functions to be performed there. There may need to be some modules at typing height, especially in a library with a small staff where the circulation desk is the major work area for everyone. On the other hand, some librarians believe that staff members at the circulation desk should be standing at all times in order to present an image of being helpful and approachable.

Both reference and circulation desks should be designed in such a manner that their function is obvious to the user. Signage may simply announce INFORMATION, REFERENCE, CHECK OUT, or RETURN. On the other hand, the shape (half-circle or U) and height (38″–40″ rather than 29″) of the desk may indicate that it is a service location. In a library or department with several desks, the material or finish may distinguish the service desks from the furnishings for the user. Or, the service desks can be "color-coded" with a finish that is different from any other in the library.

Standing-height desks are usually 38″ to 40″ high. Worksurfaces to be used by staff seated in a task chair are at a standard desk height of 29″. Most desks are built of components corresponding to other standard library furniture sizes: modules 36″ wide and desks 60″ or 72″ long. It is not unusual, however, for a library to require one or more units of another size, such as 24″, 30″, or 48″ long, in order to have the desk fit correctly into a particular space.

Tops are approximately 1¼″ thick, and are usually constructed of three-ply flakeboard. Because the worksurface must withstand hard wear over a long period of time, tops are often faced with high-pressure laminate rather than veneer. The tops can have a laminate edge; however, a solid wood edge band added to a laminate top is attractive and can be used to coordinate the look of the desk with the other wood furniture in the library.

In most cases, tops are specified to be continuous over several modules and as long as possible, considering the materials used. Since there are fewer seams on the worksurface, the desk has a more finished appearance. The individual pieces of the top are splined and held together with joint fasteners. Tops for individual units can also be specified, if desired.

The depth of the circulation desk top from the working to the public side can vary anywhere from 26″ to as much as 36″, depending on how the desk is constructed and the type of equipment that will be used on it. A desk that is built as narrow as 26″ may prove to be too small, if the equipment currently in use is 24″ deep, but larger equipment is purchased in the future. Also, one of the main determining factors in regard to the depth of the desk is the type of electrical system that is included. If the access panel to a wireway on the public side is 4″ wide, for example, the desk must be deep enough to accommodate both the check-out equipment to be used and the wireway panel.

Here is an example of how the size of the desk top should be determined: The library uses charging equipment that requires 27″ of counter space from the working side of the desk to the back of the equipment; 2″ is needed at the back of the equipment to accommodate the cords coming out of the equipment; the 4½″-wide metal wireway of the electrical system for the desk will be placed flush with the worksurface; in order to install the wireway correctly, another 1″ of worksurface will be added to the public side of the desk; finally, the desk top will have a ⅝″-wide solid oak edge band on both the working and public sides. The depth of the desk, then, should be approximately 35¾″ (27″ + 2″ + 4½″ + 1″ + ⅝″ + ⅝″ = 35¾″). (See Figure 26). In some cases, cords may go into a raceway below the worksurface through grommets. The diameter of the grommets should then be figured into the dimension of the desk top.

Circulation desks are sometimes built with wells cut out for equipment, or with the worksurface at one height and a transaction top at another height. A single-height counter top provides the maximum in flexibility when changes are anticipated in the future. Equipment can be used anywhere on the surface. Also, both the user and the staff member can slide a stack of books or other materials across the counter, rather than having to lift them to the height of the transaction top. A circulation desk with a transaction top does, however, provide a solution to the problems of shielding exposed cords from public view and from tampering. Another solution is to devise an equipment screen that fits on the desk behind the piece of equipment, such as a terminal. Ideally, the screen can be moved as the equipment is moved and finished to match the desk. It should be large enough to keep the public from tampering with the cords, but small enough to be unobtrusive. Inexpensive, ready-made screens in neutral colors can now be purchased from several of the library supply companies.

The configuration of the reference desk is an interesting design problem. If the shape is a "U," or a "fenced" square, the function of the unit is obvious,

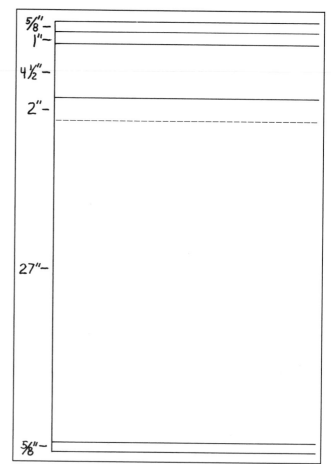

Figure 26. A sketch will help in determining the dimensions of the desk top.

but the staff is less approachable. In a service-oriented library, there is the added problem that staff members tend to stay within the confines of the desk instead of approaching the user, and may be less apt to go with the user to the catalog, shelves, files, etc., to provide extra assistance. A compromise between the two extremes of having a reference location that is a standard desk and having the staff fenced in by the desk can be accomplished. A service desk can be designed so that it has a straight, approachable front section, and two sides that are separated from the front by corner units at, for example, 30-degree angles. More than one staff member can be facing the approaching user and can easily get out from behind the desk. At the same time, the shape of the desk unit distinguishes it from any other tables or desks in the area. (See Figure 27).

Another consideration for the reference desk is the prevalent transaction that will take place there. For questions that require quick answers or moving to the catalog, the user will want to remain standing. The desk may be 29″ high on the staff side, but have a transaction top that is at standing height for the user on all, or only part, of the desk. The user may set books or other items down on the top while talking to the librarian, or the librarian may place a reference book or other information on the transaction surface in order to help the user. Sometimes a library may want a transaction top in order to hide some of the paraphernalia that accumulates at any busy desk. On the other hand, in a situation where the staff/user interaction is a long consultation about a research or technical topic, the user as well as the staff member will want to sit down. There will have to be a flat surface between them for passing information back and forth. Also, both the librarian and the user will require knee space under the desk. The kinds of equipment or special material to be used at the desk will also be determining factors in the specific design.

Another approach to take in designing a reference desk is to use components of a panel or open-office system manufactured by one of the contract furniture companies, such as Steelcase, Herman Miller, Westinghouse, or Sunar Hauserman. An advantage of these systems is that contract furniture manufacturers addressed the problems of wire management and power distribution several years ago, while the library furniture companies, for the most part, are just beginning to bring their electrical systems up to the industry standard. Another possibility with this approach is that the interior design of the library can be coordinated by using other pieces of furniture, such as study carrels and tables for computers, constructed from the same modular system. One problem with the panel systems is that they cannot be customized. Most panels are either 36″ or 42″ high. The 36″ height is too low for stand-up reference, and does not help to shield the top of the desk from public view. The 42″ height is too high for many users and staff to see over comfortably for reference purposes. Stow & Davis, now a division of Steelcase, is one company that does have a 38″-high panel that could be used with a transaction top for a reference desk.

The vertical surface on the front of service desks can be faced with a variety of materials: high-pressure laminate, wood veneer, vinyl, painted steel (some panel systems), fabric, and polyester resin. A desk is an expensive item to purchase, so the customer should expect high quality in the materials and construction. Wood veneer is frequently used on the front of the desk. The veneers should be carefully matched by color, grain, and sequence. The seams between panels should be tight.

Most libraries purchase a desk with a closed base; however, desks with an open base are also available. The Scania line sold by Highsmith, for example, has an open base. Because users will be

Figure 27. A reference center can be designed so that the staff is approachable, but not confined by the desk. Note the sloped top on the ready-reference shelves behind the desk. The desk was custom-designed by the author for Montrose Branch, Houston Public Library. Photograph includes desk and end panels made by Gayeski, sloped top made by Worden, and Estey shelving. *Photo: David J. Lund.*

standing close to the desk, a toe space that is 4″ to 6″ high and recessed 2″ to 3″ should be used to protect the bottom of the front panel on a closed base.

Several of the manufacturers now offer European-style purse or briefcase shelves on the front of the desk as an option. Another useful construction feature is a bumper rail 4″ to 6″ high. The rail extends along the front of the desk and, in effect, takes the place of the edge band on the user side of the desk. The rail extends 2″ to 3″ out over the vertical surface of the front of the desk, and thereby protects the finish by preventing users from knocking into the desk with purses, briefcases, bags, etc. A transaction top that extends out over the front of the desk serves the same purpose.

The interior units of a desk are usually constructed of ¾″ plywood or three-ply particleboard. The major library manufacturers, Adden, Brodart, Buckstaff, Gaylord, Library Bureau, McDole, Texwood, and Worden, among others, all offer a variety of modules that are standard components of charging desks. These include knee space, a card file, open storage with adjustable shelves, book return, typing desk, machine well, discharge, cupboard, and triangular or square corner units. Most knee-space units include a footrest as standard.

A high-quality desk will be finished on the interior of the units, as well as the exterior. The interior of the cabinets and the shelves should be faced with veneer or laminate. The working-side edges, as well as the edges on the public side, should have wood edge banding or be self-edged with laminate.

These standard modules should be seen as the building blocks from which a desk can be designed to fit the particular needs of the library. It is common practice for a library to specify some customized features, which can be built into the standard 36″ module. Box, file, pencil, cash, or card file drawers, for example, can be added to the basic unit. Often, drawers will be added to the top of the knee-space unit. Drawers are usually constructed with five-ply lumber core or solid wood fronts and sides. Well-made drawers have the fronts and backs dovetail joined or rabbeted to the sides. Drawers are mounted on steel, ball-bearing, and nylon full-extension slides. Service desks are finished off with end panels constructed of three-ply particleboard faced with the material used on the desk front.

In order to make the desk flexible, knee-space units can be specified with K-V track, and several extra shelves can be ordered. The knee space can then be converted to shelving, if it is needed in the future. The desk can also be built to accommodate the addition of steel storage files for specialized items such as compact discs or audio cassettes. Just as The Danish Library Design Bureau is the most innovative in shelving accessories, the company is also ahead of the American manufacturers in the type of storage units that are standard options on its charging desk. For example, DLDB has drawers available for storing audio cassettes and video tapes. Since most of the manufacturers in the U.S. will add elements to suit the customer, it is likely that they will build similar units, if the library is willing to pay the price for the custom work.

Do not assume that the library cannot afford a special feature for the desk; discuss it with the vendor. It is possible that someone else has asked for the item before. In this case, the manufacturer may have already addressed that need, or a similar one. Sometimes an item that is requested as a custom feature to a desk or other piece of furniture will become a standard option for a library manufacturer simply because it is a solution to a problem that other librarians have also noted. Once the company has done shop drawings on the item and constructed it for one customer, it is less expensive to manufacture it for succeeding customers.

Some libraries have very specialized needs in a desk. It is a good idea to do some brainstorming with the staff who will be working there to determine the detailed requirements of the design. For example, in a recently built genealogy library, the main service desk is strictly an information location because none of the material circulates. (See Figures 28 and 29). The design of the desk is especially important, because many people coming into the building have not done genealogical research before and stop at the desk to be instructed by the staff on how to begin researching their family history. Part of the instruction involves giving the new user several information sheets and forms for filling in a family tree.

Figure 28. A desk module, custom-designed by the author and built by Worden, to accommodate giveaway materials at Clayton Library, Center for Genealogical Research, Houston Public Library. *Photo: David J. Lund.*

In order to accommodate these special materials at the desk, the desk was designed to allow two librarians to work at the front of the desk. Immediately to the side of the work space for each librarian is a section of the desk that includes shelves for holding the giveaway materials. These sheets are usually 8½″ × 11″ and will never be larger than 8½″ × 14″ in size. The 8½″ width will, therefore, allow for placing enclosures three across in the 36″ module. In order to keep the items from getting lost by being pushed too far back on the shelf, a strip of wood was placed approximately 15″ from the front of the shelf. Since it was decided that it would not be necessary to have a stack of any single flyer available at any one time more than 2″ high, the retaining strip was designed 2″ high. In order to make the space flexible for other use in the future, however, the shelves were made adjustable. It is possible, for example, to remove the shelves and place several reference books in the space. (Similarly, circulation and reference desks are sometimes designed to have pigeonholes to hold smaller items that are used by the staff or given to the public.)

Most of the major manufacturers are addressing the fact that computers are now, or will eventually be, used at every desk—reference as well as circulation. The companies offer various components that can be purchased as part of individual workstation units or added to circulation or reference desks. These components include mobile or stationary printer stands, printer shelves, special accommodation for printer paper, keyboard trays or articulating keyboard arms, disk-drive storage units, turntables,

etc. Eventually, all manufacturers will have to provide a full range of options for handling computers.

Before talking to vendors, then, plan the basic requirements of the desk and make some simple sketches. Using 36″ modules as the building blocks, and special sizes where necessary, decide what will be included in each module, following this example:

> In a fictitious public library the circulation desk will face the front entrance. A person working behind the desk will see users enter the door directly in front of her/him. The main reading room will be visible to a circulation assistant looking to the right. At the left, the assistant will see the wall that separates the work area from the meeting room. One side of the circulation desk will lie against this wall, the length of which has already been determined by the architect. Considering the desk from the working side and planning in a clockwise direction, there will be two 30″ units against the wall. Both of these modules will have adjustable shelves to accommodate staff materials and books being held for users.
>
> The next module will be a corner unit. The front of the desk will include five 36″ modules. Because of the relationship of the circulation desk to the library entrance, the left side will be the return portion of the desk. The first module will be a book-return unit with a slot in the front and a depressible book truck beneath the desk. The next module will have a pencil drawer at the top and knee space below. The third unit will have two box drawers at the top (one equipped with a lock and a cash tray) and file drawers below. The right side of the front of the desk will be considered the check out and card application portion of the

Figure 29. The giveaway module in Figure 28 is part of this information desk at Clayton Library. *Photo: David J. Lund.*

desk. Going from left to right, the first of these modules will be a knee-space unit with a pencil drawer at the top, and the second will have adjustable shelves.

Next, there will be a corner unit. The right side of the desk will consist of a knee-space unit at typing height. In order to have the desk fit correctly into the space, this unit will need to be 48″ long. (See Figure 30).

The staff should also note the kinds and sizes of equipment to be used on the desk, determine the desk height and worksurface width, consider the finish desired, and note any special requirements that might be designed into the desk. This information can then be used as the basis for discussion with possible vendors. The same kind of planning can also be done for the reference desk: determine the basic requirements, decide what size modules are needed and what should be included in each section, and make some simple sketches.

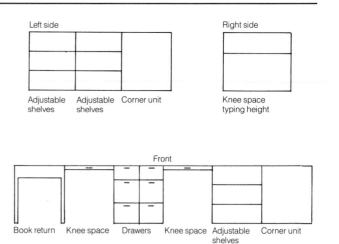

Figure 30. A simple sketch will help in planning the desk, and can be given to vendors.

Chapter 6
Chairs

No furniture item in the library receives more use and abuse than the reading chair. In a few quiet libraries, the chair may be used only for its intended purpose: to provide a place for the user to sit while reading or studying. It is not uncommon, however, for a reading chair to be dragged around the floor, to be used as a stool for reaching high places, and to serve as a temporary rocking chair for those who are more comfortable leaning back. The arms of chairs are great for those who enjoy sitting with their legs draped over something. Arms also provide a handle for the person who wishes to grab a chair and move it to a different location. In addition to allowing the traditional kind of use, the reading chair can provide seating for those who wish to sit facing the back of the chair, for those who like to sit on the backrest with their feet on the seat, and for those who prefer to sit close to the person *in* the chair, by sitting on the arm. Finally, the library reading chair can be a source of amusement for young people who like to tip backward the chairs containing their friends.

Obviously, it is essential to select a chair that is strong enough to withstand heavy and varied use. A reading chair is often expected to last for twenty years or more. In addition to being sturdy, it has to be comfortable. For many years, libraries were furnished with sturdy-looking wood- or metal-framed chairs with little style. (From an aesthetic standpoint, it is unfortunate that some of these have proven to be almost indestructible!) Now that librarians are interested in marketing library services, however, it is also desirable to select a chair that is designed to enhance the appearance of the library. If the funds are available, most libraries will choose a chair that does not look "institutional."

When selecting a reading chair for the library, keep in mind that there are a variety of kinds from which to choose: standard wood-framed library chairs, wooden captain's chairs, chairs with metal frames, stacking chairs designed for meeting or classroom use, chairs originally intended to be used as office side chairs, etc. A library chair does not necessarily have to be one that is marketed or designed for library use. A satisfactory chair may be one that is made by a contract furniture company for a much wider market than libraries.

Regardless of the manufacturer, however, it is essential to gather information about the *performance* of a chair considered for purchase. The qualities that make a chair satisfactory cannot usually be determined just by looking at it; the librarian must obtain some evidence that it can withstand heavy use and abuse over a long period of time. The price of a chair does not necessarily reflect its strength; sometimes the price may be more a reflection of the kinds of materials used to make the chair or of its perceived aesthetic value. Furthermore, the reputation of the manufacturer does not necessarily provide a good indication of the reliability of the chair for use in the library.

Information about the capability of particular chairs to withstand heavy use can be obtained in two ways. First, the consumer can contact other libraries to inquire about the reliability of the chairs. (The vendor or manufacturer should be willing to provide references to other libraries.) Second, the librarian should obtain the results of any performance tests done on a particular chair. These are accelerated-use tests that determine how well a piece of furniture may be expected to perform. Ideally, *both* performance data and the service history of the product will be available to the consumer.

Systematic performance testing and labeling of chairs and other furnishings have been done in Europe for several years. In the United States, however, performance tests for chairs are not done on a regular basis by many manufacturers; nationally accepted standards are still not developed. This is an unfortunate situation, because performance testing can benefit both the manufacturer and the consumer. The test results can be used by a company to aid in the design of improved products and to prevent possible liability suits. Furthermore, by testing sample chairs made in different production runs, manufacturers can maintain quality control. Consumers can use the results of performance testing to determine whether they are purchasing the level of quality desired in furnishings and to ensure that the most functional, durable, and safe product will be obtained for the money. When several choices are available, test results can be used to justify the purchase of a more expensive chair, if performance tests have demonstrated a longer life for the item with the higher price. In other words, the results of performance testing can be especially helpful in using life-cycle costing (also known as cost-benefit evaluation) to justify purchasing a particular level of quality.

The American Library Association began a short-lived testing program in the late 1960s as a first step toward developing standards. The formative studies of Carl A. Eckelman (Professor of Wood Science in the Department of Forestry and Natural Resources at Purdue University) were a continuation of these early efforts by ALA. His past and current research provides a foundation for the development of systematic performance testing of library chairs in the United States.

Performance testing is now done by manufacturers in in-house laboratories and by independent testing agencies, at the request of manufacturers. In addition to the data collected by Eckelman, GSA (General Services Administration) specifications provide standards that can be used for comparing the relative strength of various chairs. Manufacturers who bid on GSA projects with these specifications are required to certify that the product to be supplied has been tested, and that it can meet the GSA performance standards. The American National Standards Institute (ANSI) and Business and Institutional Furniture Manufacturers Association (BIFMA) also have standards for chairs. These are based on pass/fail tests that essentially establish only minimum standards. The tests are not as stringent as the performance testing required by GSA specifications.

Eckelman was hopeful in 1982 that manufacturers in the United States would develop a complete performance-testing system because it was in their best interests to do so. Unfortunately, this has not been the case; the development has been a very slow process. Although data are not available for some chairs, it is important that librarians know about performance testing and compare any available results in order to make informed purchasing decisions. Most manufacturers who test their products do not include this information in their literature. The librarian, therefore, should ask vendors or manufacturers whether performance data are available. As Eckelman (1982) states, "Performance tests will be conducted only if buyers and specifiers use them and only if manufacturers are assured that purchasing decisions will be based, insofar as possible, on the results of such tests and not on sudden whim." (p. 557) In other words, librarians can affect the market by basing purchasing decisions on the performance data now available, thereby forcing all library manufacturers to do testing on a regular basis.

The following discussion summarizes the points of Eckelman's reports that are most relevant to the process of selecting library reading chairs. Readers who want further background about the development of performance testing in the United States and other countries, as well as those who want to study the test results in greater depth, are encouraged to read the complete reports.

Eckelman's studies, in effect, described what happens to a chair when it is subjected to the many kinds of use noted at the beginning of this chapter. He identified eight forces that are applied to a chair by a user:

1. *Vertical seat forces* are applied to the seat of a chair when someone sits down and remains seated.
2. *Horizontal seat forces* are applied when a user pushes a chair backward, pulls it forward, slides it sideways, or tries to tilt the chair in any direction.
3. *Torsional seat loads* are forces caused by a user's changing position or twisting around in the chair.
4. *Horizontal forces on back rests* are those placed on the back rest when the user leans or tilts the chair back, when the chair is pushed forward, or when it is pulled backward and falls to the floor.
5. *Vertical forces on back rests* occur when a user slides down in the seat, tilts the chair back, or sits on the top of the back rest with her/his feet on the seat.
6. *Horizontal arm loads* are forces caused by a user pushing out on the arms of the chair when sitting down or getting up, and forces that occur when a chair is pushed or pulled sideways by the arms.
7. *Vertical arm loads* occur when a user pushes down on the arms when sitting down or rising from a chair, or when a user sits on the arm of the chair.
8. *Horizontal longitudinal arm loads* are forces that are applied along the length of the arms as someone pushes on the arms of the chair when changing positions or when sitting down or getting up from the chair. (Eckelman, 1982, pp. 509–520)

Tests that simulate these forces in the laboratory have been developed for studying the performance of chairs. Testing demonstrates how the joints and members of a chair are affected by use and identifies the components of the chair that will eventually fail. The quantitative data obtained in the tests describe the amount of force the chair can withstand without breaking. When different brands, styles, production runs, etc., are subjected to the same test, the resulting data can be used to compare the relative strength of various chairs.

Usually, the simulated action is repeated 25,000 times at a speed of 20 times per minute with the force applied at a certain load level. The force/load is then increased for the next cycle of 25,000 times, with the force continuing to increase through a certain number of cycles, or until the part of the chair to which the force is applied fails.

Eckelman's research provides some interesting performance data. In the important front-to-back-load test on seats, for example, chairs of the same style, but made by different manufacturers, were able to withstand amounts of force varying by as much as 200 lbs. Some sled-base chairs failed at loads as low as 225 lbs., while others went as high as 475 lbs. In the same test, stool-type seating (like captain's chairs) varied in strength by withstanding from 175 to 275 lbs. Four-legged chairs went from a low of 300 lbs. to a high of 400. In other words, among the products tested by Eckelman, a good four-legged chair could be almost as strong as a sled-base one; but none of the stool-type seating was as strong as the best four-legged or sled-base chairs.

The Worden Company has a well-developed program of performance testing. The data collected by the company, when combined with Eckelman's results, may very well establish the standard for library chairs. Worden's 1100 series chair (sled-base with front and back stretchers), for example, completes the front-to-back-load test at the 400-lbs. level and the vertical-load test on seats at 1,000 lbs. Similarly, the Academy chair (slat-back, four-legged chair with two side and three cross stretchers and a solid wood seat) completes the front-to-back-load test at the 400-lbs. level and the vertical-load test on seats at 1,100-lbs. In its testing, Worden has found that chairs that can withstand less than 200 lbs. in the front-to-back-load test are not strong enough for library use. On the other hand, chairs that can withstand 300 lbs. in the test have not failed with ten years of use in the library. With repeated testing, a standard for library use can be established by pinpointing more precisely the amount of force between 200 and 300 lbs. that a chair must withstand in order to give ten years of service.

Another interesting result was found in the side-thrust-load test on arms, where chairs withstood forces ranging from a low of 150 lbs. to a high of 350 lbs. As Eckelman reported, "These values are of considerable significance because they were all obtained with 'high quality' furniture. They suggest, therefore, the differences in strength that must be expected even from furniture presumably of the same quality." (Eckelman, 1982, p. 552)

The Buckstaff Company also has a complete program of performance testing that is done in-house. The laboratory has the capability of certifying products to meet GSA specifications. Buckstaff products are regularly tested to meet the *British Standard Specification for Strength and Stability of Domestic and Contract Furniture* (BS 4875: Part 1:1972). These are graded standards, with tests that establish five levels of use for chairs. Buckstaff library chairs are built to reach a minimum rating of level number four: "furniture for normal contract use, where rough treatment and careless handling occur." Some Buckstaff chairs reach level number five: "exceptionally severe contract use" (BS 4875: Part 1:1972, p. 5).

According to Eckelman, the evaluation of library chairs involves the consideration of three factors: (1) the overall structural characteristics or design of the chair, (2) the strength of the joints, and (3) the design and strength of the various members or components of the chair. All of these factors should be considered together when selecting a chair. (See Figure 31). In addition to providing valuable quantitative data, Eckelman's research generated a body of useful information that can be used in comparing the relative merits of various products.

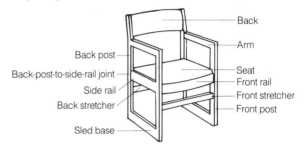

Figure 31. The members of a library chair.

Joints: A chair has joints where any two parts or members are joined, such as where the rails are attached to the legs or where the stretchers join the legs. Front-to-back-load tests on the seats of chairs demonstrate that the relative strength of one chair over another is determined more by the joints than any other component. Similar results were found in side-thrust-load tests on seats: "In chairs of essentially identical construction, chairs with well-made joints were found to be as much as twice as strong as those with poorly-made joints" (Eckelman, 1982, p. 540).

Eckelman's research found that the joint most critical to the strength of the chair is the back-post-to-side-rail joint. The testing done by Worden and Buckstaff has substantiated this. For example, Buckstaff makes a four-legged, multipurpose stacking chair that has no stretchers; however, the chair tests to meet level five of the British Standards, primarily because of a patented joint used to join the back post to the side rail. This joint consists of a unique combination of one dowel and a wedge, secured by three screws. (See Figure 32). The chair is further strengthened by the joints on the front of the chair. The front leg and rail are joined by double dowels and a bolt that threads into a slug embedded in the front rail. Mitre-corner finger joint construction reinforces the front leg and side rail connection.

Most chairs are constructed with glued-dowel or mortise and tenon joints. The particular construction of the joint is more important than the kind, however. Either a dowel or a mortise and tenon joint is satisfactory, if it is constructed correctly. Proper con-

Figure 32. Patented joint used on the Buckstaff multipurpose chair. The joint is a combination of one dowel and a wedge, secured by three screws. *Photograph courtesy of Buckstaff.*

however, testing has demonstrated that both of these types of reinforcement increase the potential for strength of the chair. Glue blocks and the bolt-and-dowel nut are standard on Buckstaff and on many Worden and Jasper chairs.

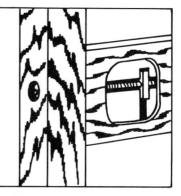

Figure 33. In addition to the primary joints, some chairs also have a bolt-and-dowel nut added where the side rail meets the back post. This supplemental construction provides assurance that the joint will remain sound even if the primary dowel joint fails.

struction can be assured by having an adequate number of dowels that are the correct size in proportion to the rails, by having enough glue that is well-applied, and by having the dowels spaced correctly. In his research, Eckelman found that satisfactory joints on a library reading chair consist of two dowels, each of which is ⅜″ in diameter and 2″ long, and which are spaced 1½″ apart. A well-glued joint is one in which "the walls of the dowel hole have been adequately covered with glue. Simply shooting a small amount of glue into the bottom of the hole in the hope that somehow it will work itself up around the dowel cannot be expected to give adequate glue coverage." (Eckelman, 1982, p. 536)

In addition to the primary joints (dowel or mortise and tenon), some chairs also have a bolt-and-dowel nut added where the side rail meets the back post. (See Figure 33). In his 1977 and 1982 studies, Eckelman considered this a supplemental construction to provide assurance that the joint will remain sound even if the primary dowel joint fails. Some chairs are also reinforced with glue blocks where the rails and legs are joined. Like the bolt-and-dowel-nut assembly, Eckelman considered the glue blocks as secondary joints to provide added strength to the chair fin the event that the primary joints (dowel or mortise and tenon) fail. Since 1982,

Rails and stretchers: The relative strength of a chair is affected by the size of the rails. The wider the front rail, the greater is the potential for strength, because the rail allows for wider spacing between the dowels. The number and size of the stretchers used also affect the strength of the chair. According to Eckelman's research, a chair with side stretchers is twice as strong as one without them, and a chair with a large stretcher is stronger than one with a small stretcher. In addition to side stretchers, front and back stretchers help to strengthen a chair, especially when it is subjected to sideways forces. On a sled-base chair, a single stretcher placed in the middle, from one side of the base to the other, helps to keep the two side frames from spreading, but does not provide the *sideways* strength of two stretchers, one on the front and one on the back.

Arms and posts: An arm on a chair serves to strengthen the chair in somewhat the same manner as a side stretcher. The arm adds to the strength, however, only if it is joined correctly to the frame of the chair. If dowel joints are used, the size and spacing of the dowels and good glue coverage are important. At the back of the chair, an arm that is attached to the front or top of the back post is stronger than an arm attached to the side of the back post. Mortise and tenon joints are sometimes used to provide a strong, attractive alternative for joining the arms of the chair to the front post.

An arm chair with a continuous front post (that is, the stump of the arm and the leg are constructed of one piece of wood) is stronger than a chair with an arm that requires a joint. In the latter case, the stump of the arm is attached to the side rail and the leg is a separate piece of wood. (See Figures 34 and 35).

Figure 34. A continuous front post and an arm that is attached to the front of the back post, rather than to the side of the back post, add to the strength of a chair. Gaylord's Informa chair is shown. *Photograph courtesy of Gaylord Bros., Syracuse, N.Y.*

Figure 35. Close-up of the arm-to-back-post joint on the Informa chair. Note the 19-ply construction of the frame. *Photograph courtesy of Gaylord Bros., Syracuse, N.Y.*

The strength of the back post of a chair is determined by the size of the post and the wood used there. The post has to be large enough to remain strong around the area of the dowel joints. The critical back-post-to-side-rail joint can be adversely affected if the back post is constructed of a piece of wood so small that the dowels from both the side and back rails meet at the same point; that is, when a relatively large amount of wood is removed in this one small area where both dowels must meet. Also, a chair with steam-bent curved back posts should be stronger than a chair with back posts cut from straight grained wood. (See Figure 36). Eckelman explains this as follows:

> If a part is steam bent from straight-grained stock, the grain of the wood tends to remain parallel to the longitudinal axis of the piece . . . . If a curved part is cut from straight stock, however, the grain of the wood tends to 'run out' of the piece . . . . This condition of the wood is commonly referred to as 'cross grain,' and parts made of cross grain wood are much weaker than parts in which the grain follows the contour of the piece. Back posts of cross grain are more likely to break if the chair falls backward, for example." (Eckelman, 1977, p. 410)

Chair style: Many different styles of chairs can be used satisfactorily in the library. The examples noted earlier illustrate that sled-based, four-legged, and other chairs can be used, if they are well constructed. Performance testing has, however, resulted in the following information about particular styles.

A sled-base chair is often selected as a library reading chair because it can be pulled up to and pushed back from a table more easily on a carpeted floor than a leg-style chair. Eckelman considered a well-constructed sled-base chair to be potentially one of the strongest available. Also, testing of four-legged chairs showed that failure occurred primarily in chairs having relatively small, square back legs.

The relative strength of the chair with the stool-type seat was found to depend on several factors: the size of the pins on the ends of the legs; the thickness of the seat and, therefore, the depth to which the end of the legs (the pins) could be inserted into the seat; the number of spindles on the back of the chair; and how well the spindles are glued. (See Figure 37).

In the testing of Breuer-type chairs with bent metal frames, it was found that cost was not a reliable indicator of the strength of the chair. The strength of this type of chair was found to be dependent on the diameter of the tubing used to construct the frame, the wall thickness of the tubing, the yield strength of the steel used in the tubing, and the location of the holes for the screws that are used to join the seat and back to the metal frame. (See Figure 38).

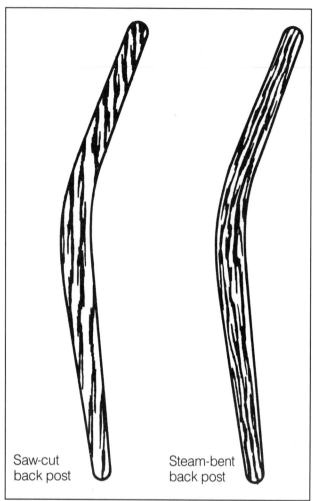

Saw-cut
back post

Steam-bent
back post

Figure 36. Curved back posts that are steam bent are stronger than those that are saw cut.

Figure 37. Captain's chair. *Photograph courtesy of Buckstaff.*

Figure 38. Breuer-type chair. *Photograph courtesy of Knoll International.*

In testing its metal-framed Diametron chair, Worden found that the gauge of steel and the type of weld used determined the strength of the chair. While a brazed joint is more attractive than a welded joint, the strongest joints are MIG (gas metal-arc) or TIG (gas tungsten-arc) welded. (Brazing is similar to soldering in that the heat used in the process does not melt the base metal as welding does. Brazing is done, however, at higher temperatures than those used in soldering.)

Based on Eckelman's conclusions, theoretically, the strongest wooden-framed library chair would be constructed with dowel or mortise and tenon joints. The dowels would be correctly sized in proportion to the rails, stretchers, and posts, and would be placed properly in relation to the other dowels used to join the parts of the chair. Specifically, the dowels would be at least 3/8" in diameter, 2" long, and spaced 1½" apart. The chair would have rails at least 3" wide attached directly to the front and back posts. The chair would have a sled base, as well as front and back stretchers. The arms of the chair would be formed from a continuous front post and would be attached to the front of the back post. If the back post were curved, the wood would be steam bent. For added reinforcement, the chair would have a bolt-and-dowel-nut construction, as well as double dowels at the side-rail-to-back-post joint and glue blocks where the legs and rails join. If it were well-constructed, this ideal chair would probably be stronger than what is needed in most libraries. The description can, however, serve as a model when evaluating existing chairs.

Salespeople representing the major library furniture manufacturers all sell a standard reading chair; however, not all of the companies manufacture chairs. Library Bureau, Texwood, and Gaylord, for example, sell reading chairs, but they do not operate chair factories at this writing. The chairs that these companies market, however, may have been designed and manufactured to be sold exclusively by them. Library Bureau and other companies have for many years sold chairs made by the Jasper Chair Company. (Another Indiana Company, JSI Jasper Seating, also makes chairs suitable for library use.) Some of Gaylord's chairs are manufactured in Europe. Adden, Brodart, Buckstaff, and Worden are examples of companies that make chairs for libraries, as well as for other markets. Some companies sell chairs made in their own factories, as well as styles purchased from other manufacturers. In some cases, it is difficult to determine which company is actually manufacturing a chair. If a chair has been performance-tested or has a satisfactory service history, however, that information may not be relevant to the selection decision. The Danish Library Design Bureau and other European manufacturers sell library chairs in Scandinavian designs made from birch or beechwood. Some of Gaylord's chairs also have beechwood frames.

The "standard" reading chair sold by library manufacturers is available either with or without arms, with a sled or four-legged base, with an upholstered seat and back, or with a wood seat and back. The chairs vary in the number of stretchers used, the placement of the stretchers, the size of the backrest and other members, and the manner in which the parts are joined. Some of the chairs have a straight backpost, while others have a slight angle at the top of the backpost and in the base frame. The seats and backs of fully upholstered chairs are typically made of bent or formed plywood. Wood seats (not upholstered) are constructed of edge-glued pieces of solid wood or of formed plywood covered with a wood veneer.

Upholstered furniture may not be as long-lasting as the all-wood chairs typically purchased in the past; however, fabric adds warmth to the environment and enhances libraries that are seeking to avoid looking "institutional." In selecting an upholstered chair, it is necessary to consider how easily the chair can be reupholstered. Seats and backs that can be easily removed for reupholstering are an advantage. In some situations customers purchase some extra upholstered seats and backs and additional material. The extra seats and backs can be used to replace worn compo-

nents on site, and the worn pieces can be sent out to be reupholstered with the additional fabric.

Manufacturers typically offer a limited, standard line of fabrics or vinyls from which to choose. Most companies will also sell items "C.O.M." (Customer's Own Material). Selecting material from another source allows for considering a wide variety of fabrics, but also adds to the cost of the item. A fabric that is 100 percent nylon is usually easier to clean and less expensive, but does not wear as well as wool. A nylon (or other synthetic) and wool blend is an attractive compromise. The padding in upholstered chairs is typically polyurethane foam.

A growing concern to the consumer, as well as the supplier, when selecting upholstery is the possible flammability hazard of the materials (fabrics and filling) used, and the resulting toxicity, if a fire occurs. A thorough discussion of the subject of flammability testing and the regulations pertaining to upholstered furniture can be found in *Specifications for Commercial Interiors* by S. C. Reznikoff, mentioned in Chapter 3. Codes are changing continually and are becoming more stringent. The most widely accepted upholstery flammability regulation for furniture is the State of California Standard (Technical Bulletin No. 116 and 117). More stringent standards include the Port Authority of New York and New Jersey and the Boston Fire Department regulations. Also, BIFMA standard F-1-1978 (Rev. A80) includes an ignition test that the GSA now requires in its specifications. Obviously, materials selected should comply with any applicable local and state codes.

The flammability regulations applicable to the materials used in a chair can have an effect on the cost. The fireproof foam required by the New York and Boston regulations, for example, can be twice as expensive as fire retardant foam required by other codes. This cost will be passed along to the consumer. The fireproof foam may also affect the comfort of the chair, since it is not as soft as fire retardant foam.

Generally, the cost of a chair is determined more by the way it looks than how strong it is. Attractive details in the styling, such as open mortise and tenon joints on the arms or bent wood frames, add to the cost of the chair. Most chair manufacturers are willing to customize a chair on request; for example, to add an arch to a standard straight backrest. That distinctive touch will, however, add to the price of the product. In bid situations requiring a sample of the item specified, it is possible that a small, local manufacturer will produce a chair that looks very similar to one made as a standard by a larger company. It is doubtful, however, that the chair will be performance-tested or have a service history. It is also not unusual for several companies to produce their own version of a chair that is popular. For example, Adden has a

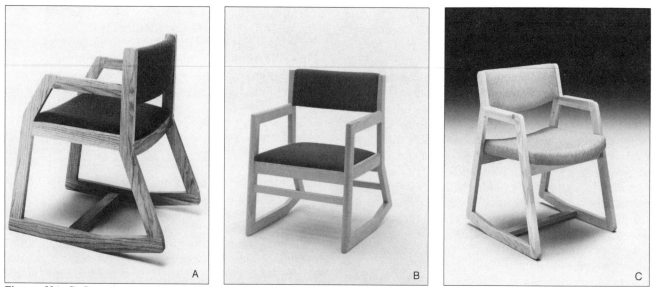

Figures 39A–C. Several companies now make a two-position arm chair. *Figure A: Photograph courtesy of Adden Furniture; Figure B: Photograph courtesy of Buckstaff; Figure C: Photograph courtesy of The Worden Company.*

dormitory chair that allows the user to sit in two positions, flat on the floor or leaning back. Recently, both Buckstaff and Worden (and possibly others) have designed and produced their own chair with this same feature. (See Figures 39A–C). Likewise, Brodart's Series E chair, Lakeland's Traverse chair, Tuohy's Lambda chair, and Worden's Anchor chair are all similar in appearance. (See Figures 40A–D).

Chairs that are not necessarily designed or marketed to be used in libraries should be considered for purchase, if funds are available. Steelcase's Snodgrass chairs (Figure 41) and Kinetic's steel-framed chairs are both sturdy and attractive designs

Figure 40A. Brodart's Series E chair. *Photograph courtesy of Brodart.*

Figure 40B. Traverse arm chair made by Lakeland Chair. *Photograph courtesy of Lakeland Chair.*

Figure 40C. Tuohy's Lambda II chair. *Photograph courtesy of Tuohy Furniture Corporation.*

Figure 40D. Worden's Anchor arm chair. *Photograph courtesy of The Worden Company.*

that can be used satisfactorily in the library. In fact, dozens of sled-based, steel-framed chairs in a variety of styles, such as those made by ICF, Krueger, Herman Miller and Rudd International can be used in a library. Breuer, captain's, and other styles of wood chairs made by a number of different companies are also used as library reading chairs.

Another choice is a steel-framed chair with a steel, wood, or molded polypropylene seat, which was designed to be a stacking meeting-room chair, made by GF, Krueger, or Steelcase, among others. (See Figure 42). These might be used in a library where chairs will have to withstand heavy student use. A high school librarian on a limited budget justified this selection sensibly by reasoning that the advantage to this type of chair is that it is made to be strong, and, if the teenagers manage to break one, it is relatively inexpensive to replace. Many other contract furniture manufacturers produce chairs that are possibilities for the library. When these chairs are considered for purchase, however, it is especially important to obtain references of long-term library (or similar public) use from the vendor or manufacturer.

There is one final consideration when selecting a chair that cannot be emphasized enough. When selecting a chair with an arm, it is absolutely essential to make sure that the arm will fit easily under the worksurface of any carrel, table, or other piece of

furniture with which it might be used. Knowing the worksurface height of that piece is not enough. The thickness of the table, desk, or carrel top and the depth of any rail or apron under the worksurface must be taken into consideration. The purchase of stylish arm chairs that do not fit under a table can be an embarrassing and costly error for a librarian.

In areas where someone is expected to sit for short periods of time, such as at a computerized catalog or at an index table, a bench or stool without a back is often used to discourage the user from occupying the position for long-term reading or studying. Stools, either leg- or sled-base, that match the frame of the reading chair are one choice. If the stool is not a standard product, it should be designed so that the members are proportioned attractively when the chair is scaled down for use as a stool. On the other hand, the construction details necessary for making a chair strong must also be present in the stool. Some possibilities for this kind of seating include the Kinetics stool with the tubular steel frame (Figure 43), and the ICF Aalto stool.

Dozens of office furniture companies, as well as library manufacturers, also make suitable lounge and side chairs. Adden, Buckstaff, Nemschoff, and Tuohy, for example, make lounge furniture with butcher block side panels. Most companies also make simple, open wood-frame styles with upholstered cushions

Figure 41. Steelcase's Snodgrass chair can also be used as a library reading chair. *Photograph courtesy of Steelcase, Inc.*

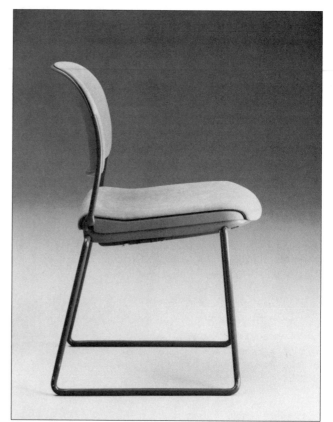

Figure 42. Some of Krueger's new line of chairs, designed by Giancarlo Piretti, are appropriate for library use. The 5500 stack chair is shown. *Photograph courtesy of Krueger International.*

and half- or full-panel chairs with upholstered side panels. Steel frame chairs made, for example, by Kinetics or Herman Miller are also used in libraries.

The same details of construction that affect the strength of a reading chair determine the strength of the frame of a lounge chair. Performance tests similar to those for reading chairs are done on lounge furniture: back frame tests, backrest foundation tests, arm strength tests, seat load foundation tests, side-thrust leg tests, and leg strength tests. The most stringent standards are those established by the heavy-duty rating for GSA Specification FNAE-80-214. This rating is equal to three 281-lb. people sitting on the sofa simultaneously (a total load of 843 lbs.) every 25 minutes, 24 hours a day, 365 days a year for ten years. Worden includes the results of these tests on many of its lounge chairs in its advertising literature. The chairs satisfy this heavy-duty rating.

With lounge seating, selection involves greater concern for the construction of the seat and back cushions than is necessary when choosing reading chairs. A common problem with a lounge chair is the tendency for the seat to sag or puddle in the center, while the rest of the chair still looks fine. Seat cushions are typically constructed of a spring unit covered with some type of foam. The cushions fail either when the springs break or the foam collapses. A unique spring design is used by Buckstaff

in its lounge chairs. The cushions are built on a double-element spring that consists of a series of steel straps and compression rods designed after the principle of the Indian longbow. (See Figure 44).

While a particular lounge chair is often selected for aesthetic reasons, the design or style of the item is also very important in determining the ease of maintenance. For example, the arms of fully upholstered chairs or sofas are likely to get soiled quickly. Better choices in areas with heavy public use are chairs with a butcher block panel that serves as an arm, or those with an upholstered side panel that has a wood strip or cap on the top of the arm, like Worden's Forum Framed series. For the same reason, a chair with an upholstered seat and back on a bent-steel or all-wood frame might be used. It is also important to consider how easily the chair can be reupholstered. Some furniture designed for offices was designed to be replaced, not reupholstered.

The design of a chair may also have something to do with how it is used. For example, librarians in facilities where a well-known style of swivel chair with a steel frame has been used have reported that children made themselves dizzy and sick by twirling around in the chair. Also, the chair should not be so low or deeply cushioned that getting up is difficult. In public areas, it might also be wise to choose a chair with few cracks and crevices where dirt can collect, and, as with the reading

Figure 45. Upholstered arms on lounge chairs used in public areas are likely to get soiled quickly. A better choice is a chair with a butcher block panel that serves as an arm, such as Buckstaff's 82 series lounge chair shown here. *Photograph courtesy of Buckstaff.*

Figure 43. Stools manufactured by Kinetics[RD] are available with a metal or fabric-covered seat. *Photograph courtesy of Kinetics Furniture.*

Figure 44. Buckstaff uses a spring design in the cushions of its lounge chairs. The construction includes a double-element spring employing a series of steel straps and compression rods designed after the principle of the Indian longbow. *Photograph courtesy of Buckstaff.*

chair, the fabric selected should be one that can be cleaned easily. In libraries where there is a large transient population, the possibility of body lice infestations should be considered when choosing upholstery.

Before making the final selection of a chair, the librarian might ask one or more vendors to supply a sample for the staff to try out. (This is a common practice in the contract furniture business.) The staff then has a chance to provide valuable input and to participate in the selection process. In summary, the selection of chairs involves answering these questions:

1. Has the chair been used successfully in similar library or other public situations for several years? And/or, is performance data available to attest to the durability of the chair?
2. Does the chair have dowel or mortise and tenon joints?
3. Are the chair rails wide enough to accommodate double dowels approximately 3/8" in diameter, 2" long, and spaced 1½" apart? How has the glue been applied?
4. Does the chair have side stretchers, or arms and a sled base that serve as stretchers?
5. Does the chair have front and back stretchers to add strength for sideways forces?
6. Does the chair have a bolt-and-dowel-nut construction at the back post and rail joint and glue blocks to add secondary reinforcement to the chair?
7. Is the chair comfortable? Are the backrest and seat deep enough? Is there enough or too much padding? Is the back at a comfortable angle in relation to the seat? (Obviously, there will be several different opinions about the comfort of a particular chair. It is a good idea, therefore, to have several different people, of varying heights and weights, try out a chair.)
8. Does the chair design and the kind of upholstery or finish used allow for easy cleaning? Can the chair be easily reupholstered or refinished?
9. Do the construction materials used meet applicable flammability standards?
10. If the chair has arms, will the arms fit comfortably under worksurfaces?

Chapter 7
Tables

Like chairs, well-made library tables should be serviceable for many years. If the library can anticipate using a table for 30, 40, or even 50 years, a substantial initial investment can be justified. A library table must remain stable in spite of being shoved or dragged from place to place, and it must be strong enough to hold equipment and books without sagging.

Different kinds of tables serve different purposes in the library; however, the elements of design and construction that result in high quality are the same, regardless of the intended use of a table. The size and number of members, the construction of the joints, and the strength of the materials used determine a table's durability. For the sake of clarity, the various elements of table construction are discussed separately in this chapter. When evaluating a table, however, it is important to consider all of its components as they relate to one another. The quality of a table depends on engineering that reflects the need for balanced construction; that is, each of the components must be as strong and as well-made as any other, so the table does not fail because of one weak element.

Performance testing of tables involves applying forces/loads in the laboratory to simulate use in the library. There are no nationally accepted tests or standards, but library tables, like chairs, can be classified according to their ability to perform under certain conditions, or when acted upon by particular forces. Tables can be compared, for example, in terms of the vertical loads they are expected to carry, their resistance to deflection (stiffness), and their resistance to sideways and front-to-back loads.

Eckelman (1977) recommends that tables be classified as appropriate for light, medium, heavy, and extra heavy duty by comparing data collected in testing various tables. He suggests that vertical loads applied to a table top be measured in terms of pounds per square foot. The ultimate load that can be supported by a table top, then, must be calculated to take into account the dimensions of the top. For example, a table 60″ (5′) long × 30″ (2½′) wide has a top with an area of 12½ square feet (5′ times 2½′ =

12½ sq. ft.); a top 72″ (6′) long × 30″ (2½′) wide has an area of 15 square feet (6′ times 2½ = 15 sq. ft.). If a heavy-duty table is defined as ultimately holding between 9,000 to 10,000 lbs., a table 60″ × 30″ would be considered heavy-duty at 850 lbs. per square foot (12½ sq. ft. × 850 lbs. per sq. ft. = 10,000 lbs.); while a table 72″ × 30″ would be considered heavy duty at 650 lbs. per square foot (15 sq. ft. × 650 lbs. per sq. ft. = 9,750 lbs.).

Resistance to deflection can be tested by measuring the amount of sag, or centerspan deflection, in a table. One criterion used frequently is that the deflection should be no more than 1/360 of the table's span. This criterion is based on the amount of deflection that can actually be *seen* (rather than measured). Sideways loads are tested in terms of the ability of the legs to withstand floor reaction forces.

Performance tests are obviously valuable in comparing the relative strength of various tables. In order to have more reliable information, however, the performance data should be related to actual use in the library. It would be helpful, for example, to know that a particular model of table 60″ long × 30″ wide, with an ultimate load-carrying capacity of 850 lbs. per square foot, has been successfully used for five to ten years in a busy library.

Eckelman identifies four types of four-legged table construction: a simple two-member cantilevered table with a top and legs, a three-member table with a top, legs, and rails; a three-member table with top, legs, and stretchers; and a four-member table with a top, legs, rails, and stretchers. (See Figure 46). Many different combinations of rails and stretchers are used, such as rails on two sides and stretchers on two sides, or stretchers on two sides and one center stretcher. Professor Eckelman cites four factors that should be taken into account when evaluating the strength of tables; his factors are listed here and subsequently discussed:

1. The general nature of the total structural support system.
2. The strength and stiffness of the legs and other supporting members.

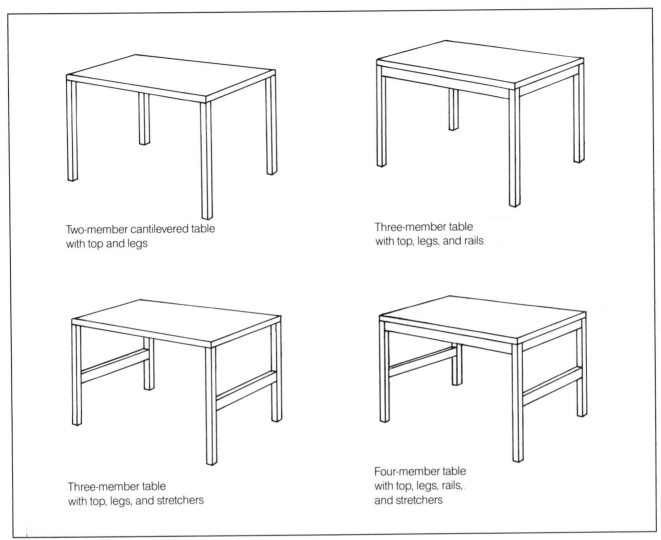

Two-member cantilevered table
with top and legs

Three-member table
with top, legs, and rails

Three-member table
with top, legs, and stretchers

Four-member table
with top, legs, rails,
and stretchers

Figure 46. Types of four-legged tables.

3. The strength and stiffness of the top and its reinforcing members (side or center rails), if any.
4. The strength and stiffness of the joints and attachments. (Eckelman, 1977, p. 367)

When evaluating tables, the following factors about the structural support systems should be kept in mind: On a simple, four-legged table, only the cantilevered legs hold up the top; there are no other supporting members. The strength of the table, therefore, depends entirely on the joints—the attachment of the leg to a steel mounting plate and the attachment of the mounting plate to the table top. Obviously, the construction of these joints should be studied carefully when selecting a table of this type. Furthermore, if a simple cantilevered table is considered for the library, references of use should be obtained and checked.

While some tables have *only* side or *only* front and back rails, full leg-and-rail construction (rails on all four sides) provides the best support for a table top.

The leg-to-rail joints provide resistance to both sideways and front-to-back forces. If the joints are well constructed and the members correctly sized, a table with rails on all sides is an excellent choice for a library. Likewise, a table with full stretchers resists both sideways and front-to-back forces. A table that has both full rails and stretchers is an extra heavy-duty table. The rails and stretchers resist both sideways and front-to-back forces. Furthermore, the rails support the top well, while the stretchers help to distribute to all four legs the weight applied to the top.

Other table support systems that may be used include the following (See Figure 48):

Leg with wooden header: The header can run either the length or width of the table. The strength of this construction depends on the quality of the leg and header assembly.

Leg with side rails: The legs are joined in pairs rather than individually. The leg-to-rail joints provide strength and rigidity to the table, but do not aid in resisting sideways forces. The durabil-

Figure 47. An oak library table with plank top and full rails and stretchers, built by The Worden Company for Clayton Library, Houston Public Library. The table is used with Worden's Academy℠ chair. The Wilson steel shelving has end panels built by Worden. *Photo: David J. Lund.*

ity of the table depends on the thickness of the mounting plates and how well they are attached.

Leg with front and back rails or legs with front and back stretchers: These tables may lack front-to-back strength, so they are sometimes reinforced with panel ends. The rails provide good support for the top along the length of the table. Again, the strength of the table depends on the quality of the joints. Tables of this type with tubular steel legs should have welded stretcher-to-leg joints to resist sideways forces. Also, the mounting plates should be of substantial size and should be strongly attached to the top.

Leg with side stretchers: Because this construction resists front-to-back, but not sideways, forces, the mounting plate must be particularly strong.

Leg with side and center stretchers: The center stretcher provides some sideways bracing, but does not provide as much strength as a stretcher-to-leg or rail-to-leg connection.

Leg with double side stretchers: The lower stretcher may actually be a sled base. This construction provides good front-to-back strength, but requires bracing for adequate sideways strength.

Leg with crossed rails or leg with crossed stretchers: These support systems are used on round or square tables and should be considered appropriate only for light duty.

The strength and stiffness of a table leg depends on its size and shape, and the materials used to construct it. Wood, for example, is not as strong or as stiff as steel, and values for strength and stiffness vary according to the wood used. (See Eckelman, 1977, p. 372, for a table of stiffness values.) The strength of a table leg can be calculated in terms of the amount of floor reaction force it can resist; however, it is unlikely that most consumers will do these calculations themselves. The service history of the product and/or performance data supplied by the

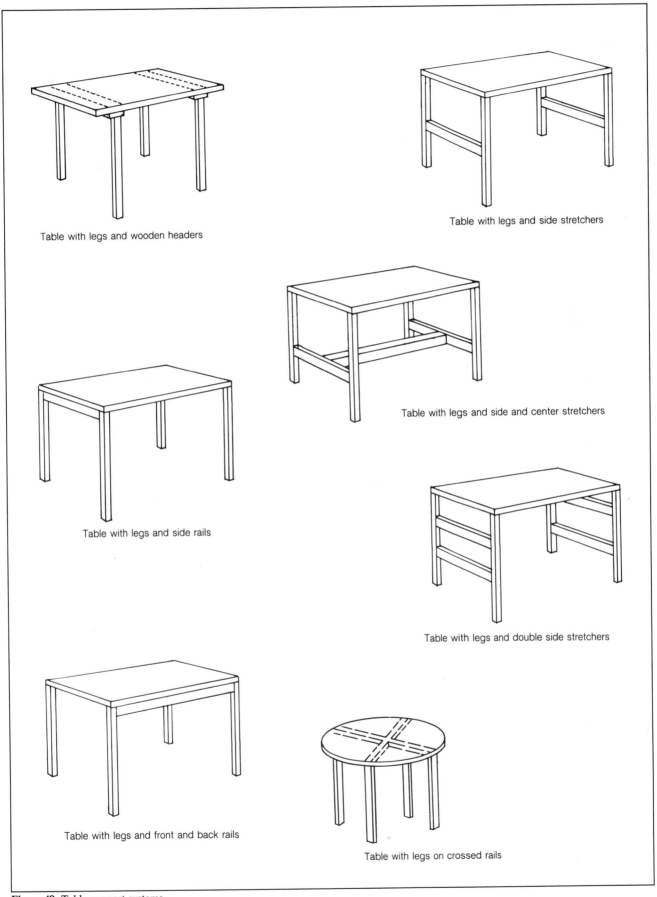

Table with legs and wooden headers

Table with legs and side stretchers

Table with legs and side rails

Table with legs and side and center stretchers

Table with legs and double side stretchers

Table with legs and front and back rails

Table with legs on crossed rails

Figure 48. Table support systems.

manufacturer should be used to evaluate the quality of a leg.

The evaluation of a table top must include the considerations concerning wood core material discussed in Chapter 3. The strength and stiffness of a table top depend on the material and type of construction used. Eckelman notes the advantages of a lumber core over a particleboard top: greater load-carrying capacity, more long-term loading strength, and less possibility of deflection. He does not, however, say that particleboard should not be used in table tops. Rather, he notes that the thickness of the top should be determined by the strength requirements of the table. It is important to know that the strength of the particleboard top is proportional to its thickness squared, so a small increase in the thickness adds greatly to its strength. For example, a top 1⅜″ thick is nearly twice as strong as a 1″ thick top. The advantage of the stiffness of lumber core does not eliminate particleboard as top material; however, when particleboard is used, it should be reinforced with side or center rails along the length of the table. In addition to lumber and particleboard cores, plywood or veneer core are used for some table tops. This material is not as strong as lumber core, but it is stronger than particleboard.

Three types of joints affect the strength of a table: (a) the leg-to-top joints, (b) the rail- and stretcher-to-leg joints, and (c) the understructure-to-top joints.

Leg-to-top joints usually involve the use of an intermediate component, a mounting plate, to which the leg is attached. With steam-bent wooden legs or steel legs, part of the leg may be bent to become the mounting device.

Sometimes the mounting plate is attached to the leg by an anchor screw that is screwed directly into the leg. All of the major library manufacturers, however, supply a stronger leg-to-top joint, which is described as being metal-to-metal. This means simply that the primary fastener (bolt or screw) does not go directly into the wood, but rather, joins the top

Figure 49. Adden's parsons table has a plank top and full rails. It is shown with Adden's arm and side chairs. *Photograph courtesy of Adden Furniture.*

and leg by screwing into a secondary metal fastener that is placed in the top or leg.

In the simplest metal-to-metal joint, the mounting plate is attached to the top and leg with bolts or screws that thread into a metal insert (bushing, Rosan, heliocoil, etc.). The metal insert is threaded into the wood itself. An even stronger construction (used by all of the major library furniture manufacturers) involves attaching the plate to the table top with bolts threaded into metal inserts as described above, and then strengthening the joint by attaching the mounting plate to the leg with one or two machine bolts that pass through the plate and thread into a steel dowel nut (or barrel nut) embedded crosswise in the leg, about 1¾″ below the plate. (See Figures 50 and 51).

Figure 50. On library tables, the legs are attached to a mounting plate with machine bolts that pass through the plate and thread into a steel dowel nut embedded crosswise in the leg. *Photograph courtesy of Buckstaff.*

Metal legs are often welded directly to a mounting plate. The quality of the weld and the thickness of the plate determine the strength of the joint. Eckelman suggests that the plate be at least ¼″ thick. The leg-to-top joint of a metal table illustrates well the need for balanced construction in a table; each part of the table must be constructed for maximum strength, so it does not fail because of one weak component.

Several different constructions are used for the rail- and stretcher-to-leg joints. One of the most common is a dowel joint. The factors that affect the strength of a dowel joint in a table are the same as those that are important in chair construction. The

Figure 51. The mounting plate is attached to the table top with bolts threaded into metal inserts embedded in the top. *Photograph courtesy of Buckstaff.*

strength depends on the size of the dowels, the spacing between the dowels, the kind of wood used, the type and coverage of the adhesive, and the tightness of fit of the dowel. The size of the dowel should be in proportion to the size of the members. The larger the size of the dowels and the wider the spacing between dowels, the stronger the joint will be. One standard that is often used is that the dowel should be at least half as thick as the thinnest of the two members that are joined together. The width of the rail or stretcher is also important: the wider the rail, the stronger the joint.

As with chairs, mortise and tenon joints are also used for tables. The tenon must fit snugly into the mortise and the amount of glue used must be adequate. When properly constructed, the mortise and tenon is slightly stronger than a dowel joint.

Wood corner blocks or metal anchor plates are also used to attach legs to rails. The wood or metal piece is attached to the leg with an anchor bolt. The block or plate is made to fit tightly to the rails by grooves cut into the rail, dadoes cut into the rail, or a full dovetail that joins the block to the rail. When used as the only joinery to attach legs to rails, this type of construction is not considered heavy-duty. Sometimes, however, corner blocks are used as secondary joints to reinforce the primary dowel or mortise and tenon joints in the leg-to-rail assembly. This construction can be considered heavy-duty. (See Figure 52).

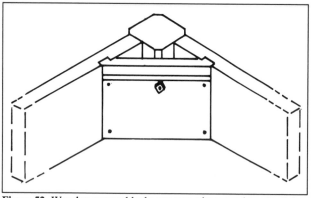

Figure 52. Wooden corner blocks are sometimes used to attach legs to rails. The block is attached to the leg with an anchor bolt and made to fit tightly to the rails by grooves cut into the rail.

In metal tables, legs are joined to the rails by welded miter or butt joints. The larger and heavier the metal tubing of the legs and rails, the stronger the joints. A miter joint is stronger than a butt joint. Also, full welding around the members results in a stronger joint than spot welding. In light- or medium-duty tables, metal legs are also bolted to rails in a type of construction that could be considered comparable to the dowel or mortise and tenon joint in wooden tables. The strength of this type of joint depends on the thickness of the metal used in the rails, the quality of any welds used in the joint, the thickness of the rail, the size and spacing between the bolts, and the strength of the leg itself. Anchor plates with anchor bolts are used in the leg-to-rail joints of both metal and wooden tables. The strength of this construction depends on the thickness of the metal anchor plate and the number and spacing of the welds used to join the anchor plate to the rail.

Stretchers are attached to the leg of a wooden table in much the same manner in which rails are attached. Dowel, mortise and tenon, or turned-pin joints (in which the end of the stretcher is turned to form a dowel) are used. As with mortise and tenon, the strength of the turned pin joint depends on the diameter of the pin, the strength of the wood, the depth of the insertion of the pin end into the leg, the snugness of fit of the pin into the hole, and the amount and coverage of the adhesive used. Stretchers are also attached to the legs with screws or with through bolts and dowel nuts. Screws and through bolts and dowel nuts are also used along with dowels to reinforce a joint.

On metal tables, stretchers may be welded to the legs or attached by some combination of screws and welded plates or tabs. The strength of the joints depends on the quality of the welds and the thickness and strength of the materials used.

Understructure-to-top joints are as important as the leg-to-mounting-plate joints in cantilever leg construction. In order to be considered heavy-duty, cantilevered tables should have steel mounting plates at least ¼″ thick. Plates ⅜″ thick are even better. The number of fasteners used and their spacing are also important in determining the strength of the mounting plate-to-top joint.

Metal-to-metal construction, rather than screws placed directly into wood, are desirable in joining the mounting plate to the top. The plate may be joined to the top by machine bolts that go through the mounting plate and into threaded metal inserts in the top, or by bolts threaded into dowel nuts (or bar nuts) embedded horizontally in the top. Another type of construction involves placing bolts through the plate into metal "T-nuts" (metal inserts) embedded in the upper side of a table. (See Figure 53). The T-nuts are then covered by high-pressure laminate. Eckelman notes that this type of construction is particularly effective with particleboard. "When installed in this way, the pullthrough strength—actually the failing strength of the nut itself—would be expected to be over 2,000 pounds. As a result, when T-nuts are used in particleboard, during laboratory tests, the corner of the table will likely break off before the T-nuts fail." (Eckelman, 1977, p. 396)

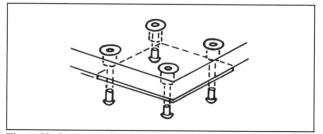

Figure 53. One type of construction involves placing bolts through a plate into metal T-nuts embedded in the upper side of the table, and covering the T-nuts with high-pressure laminate.

While the primary joints described above are critical to the strength of a table, most library tables are reinforced by the use of U- or V-shaped metal rails or solid wood keels that run the length of the table. This reinforcement is especially important on index, microform, or computer tables, which must sustain heavy loads for long periods of time.

A library usually has more than one style of table in order to make the interior more interesting, to provide users with a choice of reading stations, and sometimes, to make more efficient use of space. More round than rectangular tables, for example, can fit into a given space because the chairs of one table do not have to be placed back-to-back to the chairs at the next table.

The same library manufacturers who make wood shelving and circulation desk units also make tables. Most of them make leg-base as well as panel-end tables, which are available in several different styles and at several different prices. While each company uses a particular core material as its standard, most of them will manufacture in either lumber core or in particleboard faced with either wood veneer or high-pressure laminate. Some also make tables with a butcher block worksurface. In addition to leg-base and panel-end tables, library and contract furniture manufacturers make trestle-style tables and tables with metal or wood pedestal bases.

The leg-base tables constructed by most library furniture manufacturers use some form of metal-to-metal, top-to-leg construction like that described earlier. There are exceptions, however. Tuohy, for example, builds a sturdy and attractive parsons table with a butcher block top. (See Figure 54). The legs are attached to the top with open mortise and tenon joints. The attachment is reinforced with a countersunk, flush-plugged wood screw.

Panel ends are attached with some form of metal-to-metal joint. Most manufacturers use a wooden cleat that runs the width of the table at each end. Bolts pass through the cleat and into bushings embedded in the table top. Other bolts, placed at a

Figure 54. Tuohy's butcher block parsons table with a radius edge. Open mortise and tenon joints are used to attach the legs to the top. *Photograph courtesy of Tuohy Furniture Corporation.*

Figure 55. Panel end table, custom-designed by the author for Montrose Branch, Houston Public Library. The table was built by Gayeski Furniture Coordinates and includes Worden's electrical system. The table is used with Worden's H.E.L. sled-base arm chair. Steel shelving made by Estey. *Photo: David J. Lund.*

right angle to those screwed into the top, pass through the cleat and into bushings that are mounted on the inside of the panel end. Buckstaff attaches panel ends with a "tight" joint. (The company's standard material is lumber core.) A large "T," approximately 3″ long, is routed out on the underside of the table top on either side of the keel. The rout holds a bolt that threads into a bushing embedded in the end panel. The joint includes a heavy strip of metal, approximately 1½″ wide, through which the bolt passes in the cross portion of the "T". As the bolt is inserted, the strip of metal tightens against the lumber core in the cross portion of the T-shaped rout to hold the top firmly against the end panel. The long bolt provides support for the top, as well as joining it to the panel end. (See Figure 56).

Panel-end tables need to be reinforced with a solid wood keel or brace, 8″ to 12″ wide, that runs the full length of the table and attaches to the panel ends. Two keels should be used on tables that are 48″ wide, or more. The size of a table alone does not determine the number and size of the keels needed. How the table is used is also very important; a table that will be used to hold heavy equipment will need more than one keel and, possibly, a center support panel. Keels are attached in much the same manner as end panels. Wood cleats are placed on either side of the keel. Bolts are then threaded through the cleats into bushings in the underside of the table top and other bushings in the keel. Worden reinforces this joinery with a metal L-bracket that attaches to the end panel and to the underside of the keel at either end of the table. The attachment of the keel should involve inserting fasteners into the keel perpendicular to the grain of the wood. When a keel is attached only at the end, where fasteners are inserted parallel to, rather than across, the grain of the wood, there is a greater possibility of the fasteners pulling out or becoming loose.

Metal-leg tables are now made by several manufacturers of both library and contract office furniture. Brodart's Quantum table is a cantilevered design. A strip of metal is welded inside the top of the leg, which is attached to the mounting plate by a bolt that passes through the plate and into the metal strip. Worden's metal-legged Diametron table has a metal rail or apron. The mounting plate includes a round hub into which the table leg fits. The leg is held in place with set screws. The rails of the table fit over "tongues" that are also part of the mounting plate and are secured with screws. Kinetics and Fixtures also make metal-legged tables that can be used in the library.

Another possible option is to select a table top made by one company and specify a base from a manufacturer that specializes in selling table components, such as Berco, Redco, or Johnson Industries.

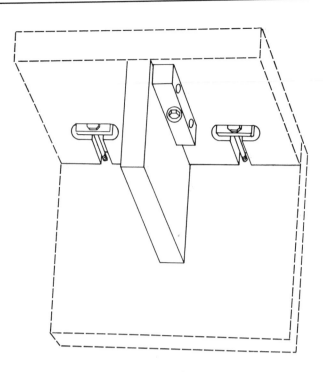

Figure 56. Buckstaff uses a "tight" joint to attach a lumber-core top to the panel ends of tables and carrels.

Bases come in a variety of styles—T-base, cylinder, disc- or trumpet-shaped, four- or five-point—and are available in colors as well as in standard metal finishes. Select a base of an appropriate size to support the top, in order to reduce the danger of the table turning over. Although it will probably not be a major concern, when choosing a table with a pedestal or T-base, keep in mind that users will naturally rest their feet on the base. For this reason, consider how well the base will hold up under this weight.

When a high-pressure laminate is used on a worksurface, the customer has a choice of using a color or a wood grain laminate that matches the wood used on the frame or base of the table. While some manufacturers claim that tables with plastic laminate surfaces are preferable in busy libraries, high-quality wood veneer or butcher block tops have been used successfully for years in many libraries. There is also no reason not to have tables with different surfaces in the same library. Wood veneer, for example, might be used on reading tables, while high-pressure laminate is used on tables holding microfilm or computer equipment. Or, wood might be used on the tables for adults and laminate used on the tables for children.

Table tops can be edged with laminate, vinyl, or a strip or band of solid wood. Laminate edges cannot be shaped like wood or vinyl, and are apt to chip or break. Several companies (e.g., Redco and Johnson) market table tops with edge bands made from highly impact-resistant plastics that are fused to the core. Wood edge bands are attractive and durable, and are available in many different shapes, ranging from a square to a full radius edge. (See Figure 57). The bands can be as thin as ⅛″ or as thick as needed. Narrow bands, ¾″ or less, are usually attached to the table edge only with glue, while wider bands are splined or tenoned and glued to the core material. The splining assures that the edge band will be positioned correctly and allows more surface for glue coverage. Gaylord's Informa series is unique in that it is constructed of nineteen-ply wood core material. No edge band is necessary because the core material itself can be shaped.

In summary, the following questions should be asked and answered when selecting a table:

1. Can the manufacturer or vendor provide performance data and/or information about the service record of the table? Can the supplier justify the design and construction of the table? (In other words, has the table been engineered to withstand vertical loads and sideways and front-to-back forces?)
2. If the table is a simple two-member, cantilevered design, are references available to verify that the critical joints are constructed well enough to keep the table from racking or wobbling?
3. Does the table have additional members—panel ends, rails and/or stretchers—to add strength to the table?
4. Are the components of the table appropriately sized to accommodate the size and number of fasteners used? For example, are the legs and rails large enough?
5. Are the joints well-constructed? Are metal-to-metal joints used to attach the leg to the mounting plate, and the mounting plate to the top, and to attach panel ends to the top and keels? Are dowel, mortise and tenon, or pin end joints used to attach rails and stretchers to legs?
6. Are the number and kinds of fasteners used appropriate for the core material? Is the core material thick enough to provide good screw-holding power?
7. Are particleboard cores reinforced along the edge with solid wood bands where necessary?
8. Is the table braced or reinforced along its length with metal rails or wooden keels of the appropriate size and number?
9. Does a very long table have center support added to keep it from sagging?
10. Is the worksurface material appropriate for the use anticipated? Can the worksurface be easily maintained?
11. Does the table have any special accessories needed, such as task lighting, electrical outlets, etc.?

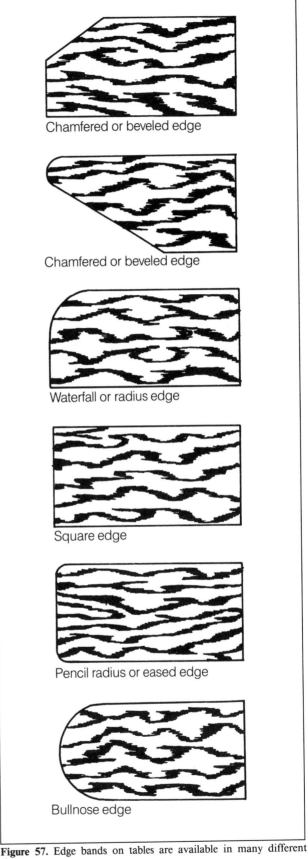

Figure 57. Edge bands on tables are available in many different shapes.

Figure 58. Many libraries prefer individual study carrels rather than tables. Shown here is Buckstaff's Cambridge series. *Photograph courtesy of Buckstaff.*

Other Library Technical Furniture

The details of construction that result in high-quality library tables are the same ones that should be used in making other pieces of technical furniture: index and stand-up reference tables, computer or microform tables or workstations, carrels and carrel tables, atlas and dictionary stands, etc. Many library users prefer individual study carrels rather than tables. Leg- and panel-base carrels are available in several styles: with full panels 48″ high on three sides, with 48″-high panels that extend along the back and about halfway across the sides of the carrel, or with a rail 4″ to 6″ high around three sides. Carrels with panels often have a shelf placed above the worksurface on the back panel, with task lights mounted under the shelf. The carrels are then equipped with electrical components to provide power for the task light and/or for equipment to be used there. Individual carrels are available in double-faced units, with two study areas back to back or as single units. When ranges of either single- or double-faced carrels are constructed, the units are purchased as starters and adders, with each range requiring one starter. Four-place carrels are also available in a pinwheel or swastika arrangement.

The attachment of the worksurface is as critical to the construction of a carrel as is the joining of a top to the panel end of a table. In many cases, the joinery is similar—bolts through wood cleats into bushings in the top and sides of the carrel. Buckstaff uses the same tight joint on carrels it uses on panel end tables. Worksurfaces are also joined to carrels with metal brackets that serve the same purpose as the wood cleats.

Librarians and manufacturers are continuing to explore the design of furnishings to accommodate computers, CD-ROMs, and microform readers and reader/printers. The challenge is to design a workstation that is functional and attractive for the items used now, but is flexible enough to allow for using different equipment in the future. In order to be flexible, the piece of furniture should be constructed with large, flat surfaces rather than several small work areas that will not allow for using larger equipment in the future. One solution to the problem of changing equipment needs is to purchase large study tables with an electrical wireway down the center. The tables can then be used either for study or work requiring equipment. Another possibility is to construct workstations using a starter/adder style, with intermediate panels between adjacent worksurfaces. Individual manufacturers have designed custom pieces to accommodate the various components of audio-visual systems and personal computers with monitor, keyboard, disk drive, and printer. Because equipment use varies so much from one library to another, it is likely that libraries will continue to require some customizing of standard items in order to have furniture that accommodates their equipment satisfactorily. (See Figures 59–62).

Figure 59. Custom-designed furniture is often purchased to accommodate audio-visual equipment, because use varies so much from one library to another. The carrel pictured here was built by Buckstaff and is available in numerous configurations. *Photograph courtesy of Buckstaff.*

In spite of the increase in computerized and microfilm catalogs over the last few years, librarians are still buying card catalog cases. All of the library furniture manufacturers continue to make card catalogs. Most catalog trays are now plastic rather than wood. The craftsmanship required to construct a wood catalog tray with full dovetail joints makes the wood trays too expensive for most libraries to purchase. Library Bureau, a name that has long been a standard in the field, continues to sell substantial numbers of card catalogs, as older libraries add cases or new libraries purchase furnishings. Library Bureau still offers wood card catalog trays, as well as the plastic ones.

Card catalogs are available with leg- and full- or open-panel bases. The cases are made in vertical styles 60″ or more high and "range" or "rancher" styles, 40″ to 45″ high. Card catalogs can be purchased as a unit or in modular sections. There is no standard size for catalog cases. If the library plans, therefore, to add cases some day, it would be best to select initially a standard product from a manufacturer who has a history in the business and is apt to be around in the future. Catalog cases made in special sizes or with special finishes can become a problem. Custom work may be affordable when purchasing the initial catalogs because of the quantity involved, but when a smaller number of pieces are needed later, the custom work involved may be very expensive.

Well-constructed card catalogs will last for years. All of the elements that determine quality in the wood construction of other library furnishings are applicable to catalog cases: the materials used, the kinds and construction of joints, and the overall support system. In addition, a high-quality card catalog has the following attributes:

1. The trays move easily in and out of the box openings and are interchangeable with any other trays in that unit.
2. The side rails for the trays are constructed of solid wood, so they do not wear away with the friction of the moving tray.
3. The wood drawer fronts are attached to the plastic trays with a joint that imitates the dovetail or rabbet in all-wood cases.

Figure 60. Computers, CD-ROMs, and microform readers can be used on tables designed for such equipment. This table was custom-designed by the author for Helen Hall Library, League City, Texas, to hold a computerized catalog. The library also has double-faced, stand-up tables of the same design. The tables and 1100 series stools were manufactured by Worden. *Photo: David J. Lund.*

Figure 61. At Irving Public Library, Irving, Texas, the card catalog *case* will eventually become the *table* to hold the computerized catalog. Notice the electrical system in the table top. The cases/tables were made by Worden. *Photo: David J. Lund.*

4. The hardware on the drawer front is metal, rather than plastic.

5. The case is adequately supported and does not sag in the middle. (Keels or intermediate panels are used to provide extra support for leg- and open-panel-base cabinets.)

6. Sliding reference shelves are constructed of wood, rather than plastic, so they will not bend or break.

Wooden book trucks are usually purchased along with library furnishings. All of the major library manufacturers make them. Although they are subjected to very heavy use and abuse, a good wooden book truck should be serviceable for many years. A poorly constructed book truck is difficult to maneuver, becomes wobbly as the joints and wheels fail, and is more apt to tip over than a well-made truck. The book truck should be constructed of lumber core or solid edge-glued lumber. On high-quality

trucks, the shelves and end panels are connected with mortise and tenon joints; the underside of the shelves are reinforced with glue blocks. Rubber bumpers specified on the sides and the bottom shelf of the truck will help to prevent damage to walls, shelves, etc. when they are bumped by the truck. Most trucks have two swivel and two stationary wheels. For stability, the wheels should be five inches in diameter. Library Bureau makes a particularly sturdy book truck that is mounted on very heavy-duty cast metal casters.

Children's Furnishings

Throughout this discussion, the emphasis has been on selecting items that can withstand heavy use from "the public": local residents, high school and college students, or the staff of a company. The ultimate testers of library furniture, however, are

Figure 62. Workstations can be built in a starter/adder style with intermediate panels between worksurfaces. Notice that each microform reader station has a pull-out writing shelf that is flush with the trim edge of the table when it is pushed in. Tables are also available with writing shelves for left-handed users. Steelcase Sensor chairs are used here. The workstation configuration was designed by the author for Clayton Library, Houston Public Library. The tables were built by Worden. *Photo: David J. Lund.*

young children. The market for children's library furniture is not very large. Children's furniture is made by companies that serve libraries generally and, sometimes, by companies that serve the contract office furniture market as well. At the present, several companies are making high-quality furniture for children's areas; however, this has not always been the case, nor will it necessarily continue to be the situation in the future. Because the market is small, children's furniture is sometimes a target for elimination when a manufacturer cuts back a product line. For example, Stendig and Rudd International once had excellent lines of children's furniture. Unfortunately, what is available today may not be here tomorrow.

At one time, library chairs and tables for children were merely cut-down versions of the standard chairs and tables for adults. Little attention was paid to the need to proportion the members of chairs and tables as they were redesigned for young people. The major

library furniture manufacturers, however, have become more responsive to the need for better, more attractive products for children in the last few years.

It is very important when selecting children's furniture to research use of the product. Obtain the service history of the product by talking to librarians who have used the items under similar conditions. Even heavy schoolroom use does not equal the amount of unintentional abuse to which a children's chair in a public library is subjected. For example, one library selected a very expensive European line of plastic children's furniture that was promoted as being able to withstand use in a busy classroom for preschool youngsters. The tables and chairs looked indestructible; however, they all were destroyed by "normal" use in the public library within a couple of years' time. Also, juvenile furniture is not used only by children. Any seating for children should be capable of providing seating for adults as well.

Figure 63. Class Act 14 children's chair made by JSI-Jasper Seating. *Photograph courtesy of JSI.*

Figure 64. Gaylord's juvenile stacking chair. *Photograph courtesy of Gaylord Bros., Syracuse, N.Y.*

Too often, the toddlers, the ones who seem most to enjoy climbing on a chair just their size, are neglected, as librarians compromise on larger furniture in order to have only one style. If funds are available, it is preferable to have more than one size of furniture in the juvenile area: very small tables and chairs near the picture book shelving for toddlers and preschoolers up to the age of three or four, and larger furnishings for youngsters between the ages of five and eight or nine. In some cases, a third

category of users, young adults, might be distinguished also.

The youngest library users should have tables approximately 20″ to 22″ high and chairs with a seat height of 12″ to 14″. The older children will require tables about 24″ to 26″ high and chairs with a seat height of 15″ to 16″. Some young adults areas are furnished with a chair of standard adult height used with a table 26″ or 27″ high, rather than the standard adult height table of 29″. Just as with adult furniture, if the chairs have arms, it is imperative to make sure the arms will fit comfortably under the worksurface. Also, make sure there is ample leg room between the seat of the chair and the underside of the table.

Figure 65. Traverse child's chair by Lakeland Chair. *Photograph courtesy of Lakeland Chair.*

The strength of a chair for children depends on the same construction features that determine the strength of an adult chair. The chairs can be all wood or have an upholstered seat and back. Another possibility is an all-wood seat with an upholstered backrest. Fabric or vinyl upholstery is sometimes chosen over wood because it adds color to the area. There are, however, other ways in which furniture can help to make the children's section colorful. For example, chairs and tables manufactured by Nemschoff have wood frames stained in bright colors. The frames can be used with matching vinyl upholstered seats. The Danish Library Design Bu-

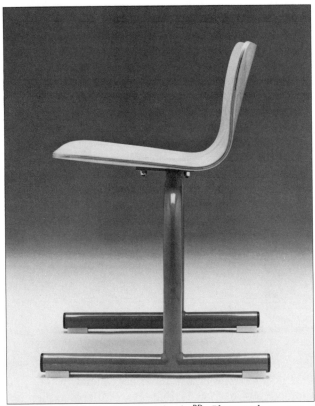

Figure 66. Children's chair by Kinetics[RD]. *Photograph courtesy of Kinetics Furniture.*

reau sells a versatile and attractive line of furniture, named Jysky, that is manufactured and performance-tested in Finland. The chairs, tables, stools, and other items come in several different sizes and are made of solid birch. Both table tops and chair seats are available in several colors. Chair frames come in natural birch or can be painted. Gaylord offers a juvenile stacking chair with a natural finish birch frame and a red, molded, wood seat and back. Another possibility is the Aalto multi-section table and chairs manufactured by ICF (International Contract Furnishings, Inc.). ICF also has an Aalto stool with a bent-knee leg that is available in a children's height. The frame of the stool is natural birch. The seats of the chairs and stools and the top of the multi-section table are available in brightly colored plastic laminates.

Adden, Brodart, Buckstaff, and Worden are some of the library manufacturers who make sturdy tables and chairs for children. In addition to the juvenile stacking chair, Gaylord sells a line of solid oak chairs for children. JSI-Jasper Seating and Jasper Chair Company also make children's chairs. Highsmith sells children's tables and chairs of beechwood as part of its Scania line. Worden makes both its stylish H.E.L. and Diametron chairs, as well as other designs, in children's sizes. Tuohy manufactures a sturdy children's chair that has a frame based

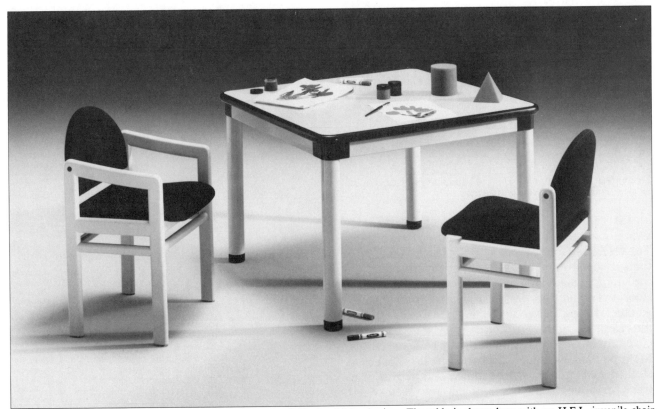

Figure 67. Worden's Diametron™ tables and chairs are available in children's sizes. The table is shown here with an H.E.L. juvenile chair. *Photograph courtesy of The Worden Company.*

Figure 68. Metropolitan Furniture offers children's tables and chairs made with steel frames encased in textured rubber tubing. *Photo: Burns and Associates.*

Figure 69. Kinetics Scamps[RD] children's furniture is made of tubular steel. *Photograph courtesy of Kinetics.*

on the Lambda adult chair. This chair is similar in style to Worden's Anchor juvenile chair and the Traverse child's chair made by Lakeland Chair. Although stools may not be standard items, most of the library manufacturers will make a children's stool based on the design of one of their chairs. Another strong possibility is Kinetic's Scamps furniture, made of heavy tubular steel with laminate-covered seats and backs and brightly colored frames. Metropolitan Furniture Corporation also makes a steel-framed children's chair in two seat heights. The black, powder-coated frame is encased in textured rubber tubing. The seat is available with a textured finish, in clear-lacquered beech, or upholstered. A Canadian company, Group Four Furniture, manu-

factures arm and armless children's chairs in two seat heights. The chairs have bent-metal frames and molded plywood seats that are available either upholstered or in a natural birch veneer.

Figure 70. Jysky children's furniture is imported from Finland and sold by The Danish Library Design Bureau. *Photograph courtesy of The Danish Library Design Bureau.*

Several companies (Adden, Brodart, Gaylord, and Highsmith, for example) also sell soft-sided or bean bag children's seating, or close-to-the-floor

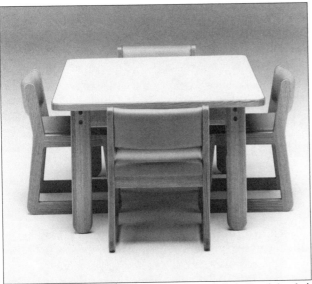

Figure 71. Tuohy makes a small version of their Lambda chair that can be used with their children's table. *Photograph courtesy of Tuohy Furniture Corporation.*

Figure 72. Nemschoff makes sturdy furniture for children. The chairs are available with frames stained in bright colors to match vinyl upholstery. *Photograph courtesy of Nemschoff, Inc.*

cushions in a variety of shapes. The cushions or seats are filled with polyurethane foam or styrofoam pellets, and are covered in brightly colored fabric or vinyl.

All of the companies that make chairs also make tables; squares, rectangles, rounds, and other shapes are available in one or more heights. Half-rounds are also used in combination with a square or rectangle to make an oblong unit that can be pulled apart into several smaller tables. Several companies also make picture book tables with slanted tops and matching benches. Laminate tops with a wood edge band, laminate self-edge, or a vinyl edge are standard on children's tables. Attractive metal-leg tables are also available for children. Metropolitan and Group Four Furniture, for example, have round and square tables that coordinate with their chairs for children. Worden's Diametron tables, and some of Kinetic's 400 and 700 series tables, have round metal legs that come in bright colors, and that can be coordinated with the other furnishings in the area, as well as with the plastic laminate table tops.

Chapter 8
Task Furniture

While users are aware of library employees who check out books or answer questions at the reference desk, the librarians or members of the support staff who are playing a vital role *away* from public view are often forgotten or ignored. A representative of a major library supply firm recently revealed an unfortunate, but not uncommon, lack of understanding of the wide range of library functions when he stated that a library does not have the power distribution and wire management requirements of a general office. While there is a difference between contract office furniture and most items manufactured for use in the *public* section of the library, furnishings used by the staff in workrooms and technical services areas are the same as those used in any office.

Like other businesses, libraries are in various stages of transition from conventional to automated offices. Unfortunately, funds are often not available for completely refurbishing an office area to accommodate new equipment and procedures. Administrators recognize the necessity for allocating funds to purchase furnishings for public areas; expenditures for these items will be readily noticed by those receiving service or those responsible for funding. Staff members, therefore, often receive the short end of the proverbial stick and may be left with makeshift workstations, odds and ends of furniture, and jerry-built power distribution. In many libraries, technical services functions are allocated inadequate space. Staff members are forced to share much of their work area, and have little privacy and definition of their "territory." So many tasks are going on in one small area that noise and distraction are common problems.

Librarians with funds for renovating work areas or building new facilities have a unique opportunity to furnish space that will accommodate the automated office now and in the future. Furthermore, they have an obligation to their organization to take advantage of current knowledge of human factors in the workplace by designing work areas that are comfortable as well as functional, and that contribute to the productivity of the employee.

The subject of furnishings for the workplace is too extensive to be covered comprehensively here. We can, however, point out the importance of making thoughtful decisions when purchasing task furniture, and provide some suggestions about the questions that should be posed to vendors about their products. Just as with furnishings in the public area of the library, life-cycle costing of the products to be purchased for the workplace should be considered. A little more money spent on the initial investment of furnishings can save hundreds of dollars in replacement costs in the future. Task furniture—chairs, desks, files, etc.—should be serviceable for ten to twenty years or more.

An excellent book to consult is *Designing the Automated Office, A Guide for Architects, Interior Designers, Space Planners and Facility Managers* by William L. Pulgram and Richard E. Stonis. Anyone involved in planning an office area is advised to read the entire text. In addition, Chapter 12 of *Specifications for Commercial Interiors* by S.C. Reznikoff is relevant to office planning.

Most libraries have open office areas for technical services and support functions; the individual workstations are not enclosed by walls that run floor-to-ceiling. Usually, only administrative and supervisory staff are assigned office space that is fully enclosed. Work areas can be furnished with conventional freestanding furniture (desks, tables, lateral or vertical files, and credenzas), with furniture that is part of an office panel system, or with a combination of freestanding and system furniture. The concept of system furniture is one that is familiar to librarians who are accustomed to working with shelving and other items constructed in 36″ modules. Panel systems define individual work areas and make the most efficient use of space by utilizing modular components available in fixed sizes (worksurfaces, file and box drawer pedestals, and overhead storage compartments).

Decisions made in designing work areas and selecting the furnishings should be based on a clear understanding of: (1) personnel, space, work flow, and equipment needed for the tasks to be performed in the work area now and (2) possible growth and changes needed in the size of the staff, space, equipment, and tasks to be performed in the future. Any library that is planning or redesigning a work area should conduct a workplace audit to gather the information needed to make sound decisions. (Representatives of major contract office furniture manufacturers will provide direction and assistance in performing an audit and planning a work area, if you are seriously interested in their product.)

In a major renovation or building project, it is the reponsibility of library personnel to provide the architects, engineers, or other design professionals with the information collected in the audit so that work areas will be planned correctly. The details of building design—power distribution into and throughout the area, acoustics, lighting, HVAC (heating/ventilating/air conditioning), and the structure itself—are crucial to the success of work areas. Mistakes in designing these elements may cause costly problems later. Poorly designed workspaces (or makeshift accommodations) have one or more of the following: lighting that is inappropriate for computer use or other tasks; inadequate acoustical treatment of noisy areas; dangerous and unsightly power distribution involving extension cords, cables taped to the floor, dangling wires, and power poles; and HVAC that does not provide a comfortable environment for the staff or correct conditions for proper maintenance of equipment. (See pages 96–99 of Pulgram and Stonis's *Designing the Automated Office* for excellent checklists of "Environmental Concerns of Building Systems" and "Health and Safety Considerations.")

Data collected in surveys performed by Louis Harris and Associates for Steelcase (published in 1987 and 1988) point out the importance of providing appropriate furnishings for work areas. The studies identify the following elements of the office environment that are of concern to staff: adequate work-surface space, appropriate storage and filing, seating, proper lighting, privacy, freedom from distractions and noise, and a comfortable temperature in the workspace. It is especially interesting to note that "sixty-one percent of office workers—up from 45% in 1978—feel it's very important to have the work-surface, chair, storage space and other furniture needed to get the job done well." (Steelcase, *The Office Environment Index. 1987 Summary Report*, 1987, p. 14.)

Many companies manufacture and sell office furnishings. The quality of the furniture varies greatly; therefore, it is extremely important to have information about the manufacturer of the products selected for purchase. Furthermore, the parts of office systems, chairs, and freestanding furnishings are not standardized among manufacturers, so in order to get replacements for lost or damaged parts in the future, you will have to deal with a company that is still in business. It is important, then, to know whether or not the company you select has been making office furnishings for a number of years and is likely to be around for several years to come. One key to this information is the warranty offered by the company. A company that offers a five- to ten-year warranty should be considered more reliable than one that offers only a one-year warranty. The reputation of the manufacturer is also important. The giants in the industry are well-known and the service history of their products is readily available. Other indications of the reliability of the manufacturer include the following: (1) the company is involved in new product development that demonstrates customer-responsiveness and a commitment to technology; (2) the manufacturer has a continuous program of quality control and product performance testing; (3) the products are readily available from reliable dealers who provide satisfactory installation, user training when necessary, and service after the sale.

The same considerations of function, maintenance, and appearance that are used to select library furnishings for the public area are used in choosing task furniture. Aesthetics is a secondary issue in selection, while function and maintenance are of primary importance.

The overriding concern when selecting functional items for the automated office is that the furnishings, as well as the work space, provide maximum flexibility. The furnishings selected play a vital role in ensuring that the space will have the flexibility to accommodate future changes and provide the environment desired by the staff.

Modular panel systems or a combination of panels with freestanding furniture provide the flexibility needed in the automated office. Furniture systems also accomplish the following: define personal work space, provide privacy, alleviate some of the problems of distractions and noise, aid in the organization of work, direct communication between particular staff members, and allow for time-sharing of equipment. Panel systems are designed to make the most of the vertical space in each workstation. Spaces can be reconfigured, enlarged, or reduced as tasks are reorganized.

Many elements of function and maintenance should be considered when selecting a flexible workstation. Talk to the representatives of several manufacturers and compare the systems before selecting one. All of the following questions are relevant. (The word *system* in the questions below refers to any type of modular workstation, regardless of whether it contains freestanding units, components of a panel configuration, or a combination of both.)

1. Does the system allow for adjusting the height, position, or angle of the components of the workstation?
2. Does the system allow for expanding and contracting the size of the workstation? Can workstations be easily adapted in shape?
3. Is a variety of module options and configurations available? Are both freestanding and systems components available from the same manufacturer?
4. Do drawers and files come with inserts necessary for using them immediately for either legal- or letter-sized filing or other storage ? Or is it necessary to purchase additional hardware in order to use the items?
5. Can additional components be added to the initial installation? Does the system allow for retrofitting pieces?
6. Does the system provide wire management and adequate power, data, and telecommunication distribution with the capability for accommodating future technological changes? Is a variety of options available in regard to handling power and communication in the system?
7. Does the system have the simplicity and flexibility of design to allow for ease in dismantling and relocating workstations?
8. Are the components from one module of the system interchangeable with other components of the same system?
9. Is the system designed to allow easy access to areas or components that might require servicing?
10. Are replacement parts readily available?
11. Are the construction materials and finishes desired available? Can materials and finishes be easily maintained?
12. Is the system designed for strength and stability? Can the manufacturer provide performance data or other evidence that worksurfaces will not sag? Does the support for cantilevered worksurfaces extend the full depth of that surface? Can box drawers and files hold the weight of materials to be stored there?
13. Is the system designed in such a manner that panel-mounted components can be installed easily? Does the panel allow for attaching brackets (which support the components) into slots placed every 1″ to 1½″ along a vertical channel? Do the brackets which attach to the panels lock securely in place?
14. Do drawers or doors operate smoothly and conveniently?
15. Does the system make the most of the vertical space available on the panels? For example, are drawers or files under the counter as deep as the worksurface?

When selecting a workstation, a number of questions concerning the effectiveness of the item from the standpoint of the user should also be answered:

1. Does the workstation allow for ease of movement from one task to another, or from one part of the station to another? Is clearance from the underside of the worksurface to the floor adequate?
2. Does the workstation provide ready accessibility to items needed to complete tasks? Does the computer or other equipment get in the way of performing some tasks?
3. Do the components of the workstation provide a convenient area for accomplishing all necessary tasks? Is the workstation the right size, shape, and depth to accommodate equipment?
4. Does the workstation provide appropriate lighting for all tasks, and proper viewing distance and angle for using the computer or other equipment?
5. If necessary, does the workstation allow for the completion of individual tasks as well as conferencing?

There are dozens of manufacturers of furniture systems. A few of the major ones are Corry-Hiebert, Haworth, Herman Miller, Knoll, Steelcase/Stow & Davis, Sunar Hauserman, and Westinghouse. These companies make high-quality panel systems constructed mainly of steel, with some wood members or wood veneer surfaces. The structural panels that define workstations and support the components of the system are available in several widths and in a variety of heights, ranging from approximately 34″ high to ceiling height. Acoustical panels are frequently used in open office situations to aid in noise reduction; however, glass, vinyl-clad, or veneer- or laminate-faced surfaces are also used on panels. The trim or caps on the panels are available with painted or fabric-covered surfaces. Caps of chrome or wood are also available. The panels support the brackets used to mount the components of the workstation, and contain the channels for handling wire management and power, data, and telecommunication distribution throughout the unit. The panels allow for configuring and clustering workstations in many, many ways.

If a manufacturer sells freestanding furnishings as well as office systems, the freestanding units can be used along with modular components. This combination allows for moving the freestanding units to some other location, such as into a closed office, and reconfiguring or adding components to the original workstation. Freestanding units and system components are available with either painted or wood veneer finishes on the vertical surfaces.

Figure 73. Wood and steel panel systems made by contract office furniture manufacturers can be used in many areas of the library. An Ethospace® interior made by Herman Miller is pictured here. This flexible system consists of detachable tiles in steel frames. *Photograph courtesy of Herman Miller, Inc.*

A variety of sizes of worksurfaces (including corner units) are available. Worksurfaces are constructed of particleboard or steel-core (depending on the manufacturer) faced with either veneer or high-pressure laminate. Worksurfaces can be placed at varying heights, to accommodate several different tasks. Other components of the systems include pedestals that carry box and file drawers, and overhead storage compartments in several different sizes. Task and ambient lighting are available as part of the systems. Many accessories and components that aid in the use of computers, such as articulating shelves for keyboards and paperflow trays, are now part of the systems.

In addition to the full line of panel systems and conventional units offered by the manufacturers of steel office furniture, some companies sell items designed specifically to support computerized functions. These furnishings include straight and curved word processor workstations, mobile pedestals, individual computer tables with dual-height worksurfaces to accommodate the keyboard and the termi-

nal, printer stands, and mobile terminal stands. Some of these specialized furnishings are designed to be flexible with such features as height-adjustable worksurfaces; extendable keyboard platforms that can be used to adjust the eye-to-screen distance for the computer user; and keyboard and terminal platforms with adjustable tilt mechanisms and height-from-floor adjustment capabilities. Many accessories for use with computers are also available, such as locking security cabinets for computer equipment, foot and palm rests, carousels for holding equipment shared by adjacent workstations, and document holders.

Many companies are now making panel systems and/or individual work units for automated offices primarily of particleboard faced with laminate. These products are less expensive than the steel and wood furnishings made by the companies carrying full lines of office furniture. They have many of the adjustability features of the more expensive products and may be acceptable where only one or two units are needed. For a major project where furnishings

Figure 74. This panel configuration combines Stow & Davis Elective Elements with Steelcase 9000 series freestanding furniture. *Photograph courtesy of Steelcase/Stow & Davis.*

will be purchased in quantities, and where the items are expected to last many years, the relevant check questions regarding wood construction (p. 20) and workstations (p. 74) should be answered in deciding which product to purchase.

Another possibility for furnishing automated work areas is using computer workstations now being manufactured by some of the library furniture companies. Since much of the traditional furniture manufactured for libraries is modular, it is not surprising that these companies have developed panel systems with components built to accommodate computer use. Printer enclosures and stands, work-surfaces with keyboard trays, turntables for shared-computer use, and mobile pedestals are some of the products now available. As automated functions increase, customer-responsive library manufacturers will probably expand their lines of this specialized furniture, especially if these items can be sold as part of a complete furnishings package for new or renovated buildings.

Just as dozens of manufacturers sell desks, panel systems, and workstations, dozens of companies also sell chairs for offices. A recent issue of the trade magazine *Interiors* has pictures of over 25 different chairs for office use—and these are only the more expensive, high-quality products.

When selecting office chairs, it is again essential to choose a manufacturer that has been in business a long time, is apt to remain in business, and has a reputation for being one of the leaders in the office furniture industry. Some of these companies are

Herman Miller, Knoll, Krueger, Steelcase, Sunar Hauserman, and Vecta. (See Figures 75–80).

It is interesting to note that a high-quality chair is not necessarily the most expensive one. It is possible to buy a chair that will last for ten or twenty years and pay less for it than for a chair that is not as comfortable and will not last as long. The price is often based on the way a chair looks—its aesthetic appeal—rather than on functional considerations. It is also important to remember that even very inexpensive office chairs in a high-tech style may look good when they are new, but if the chairs soon fall apart or have broken parts that cannot be replaced, they are no bargain.

It is a well-accepted fact that comfort is vital to employees who spend a relatively large part of their working hours in a chair at a desk, often working with a computer, typewriter, or other piece of equipment. It is difficult to find a work chair that will please everyone on the staff. With so many options available, however, it is important to try out several chairs, talk to more than one dealer, check references, ask about performance testing, and, possibly, get some advice from a designer or consultant.

All manufacturers of work chairs use the word "ergonomic" somewhere in their advertising, referring to the aspect of technology that is concerned with the application of biological and engineering data to problems relating to people and machines. The word has been used so much that it no longer distinguishes one product from another. The use of computers in offices (lots of time spent in a chair looking at the screen) and an increase in research on the human engineering factors of office work have contributed to the development of chairs that are better for the body and are more comfortable. Take advantage of this development and select a chair that has the benefit of good engineering behind it.

A high-quality office chair should have the following attributes:

1. The size and design of the backrest should allow for proper back support and distribution of the user's weight and correct curvature of the spine. The chair back should allow for differences needed in the height, angle, and tension of the backrest for different people.

2. The chair should be designed and contoured properly in order to distribute the user's weight and support the body correctly.

3. The seat should be shaped and angled to position the spine properly and distribute the user's weight correctly. The front of the chair should have a radius edge that will not cut into the leg of the user. The chair seat should have enough foam to make it comfortable.

4. The arm should be designed in such a manner that it does not impede movement of the user from side to side. The arm should also allow for pulling the chair under the worksurface.

5. The chair should have a five-point steel base for stability. The base should be designed to minimize interference with the feet and legs of the user.

6. The chair should allow for height adjustment, either manually or with a pneumatic lift, so the user's feet can rest flat on the floor.

7. There should be a "family" of chairs available in a particular style to allow for purchasing chairs for different tasks and different levels in the organization (manager's or executive's chairs, operator's or task chairs, secretarial posture chairs, high swivel stools, and side chairs). Preferably, the chair will be available with seats of more than one dimension to allow for differences in the size of users.

8. Several different choices in the kind of casters for the chair should be available. The purchaser should specify the caster that is appropriate for the floor on which the chair will be used. The chair should maneuver easily, while still allowing the user to maintain control.

9. The chair should allow for ease of reupholstering. Service and parts for broken chairs should be readily available.

Several years ago, manufacturers recognized that more than one person may use the same chair in an office. In order for a chair to be comfortable for people of different sizes and tastes, it has to be adjustable. Office chairs were designed, therefore, with several points of adjustment which could be controlled by knobs, levers, or buttons. Many of the chairs now on the market are of this design.

The reason for having adjustable chairs is valid; however, busy employees often will not take the time to make the adjustments. Furthermore, if using the chair correctly is so complicated that it requires hands-on training, many people don't want to bother with it. The best chairs developed recently recognize the need for adjustability and are engineered to support the body properly. They do not, however, require a number of adjustments by the user. The manufacturers call the chairs self-adjusting, or say that they provide for passive adjustment. These chairs are designed and engineered to conform to the body of the user as much as possible, without the user actually having to adjust some part of the chair.

One of the best examples of the self-adjusting chair is the Sensor chair manufactured by Steelcase. The chair has a flexible, one-piece polypropylene inner shell that is designed to support continuous movement and to flex with the body. The angle of the seat is self-adjusting, and the chair is contoured to eliminate the need for height adjustment of the backrest. The only two adjustments controlled by the user are the height and tilt tension. The chair is designed to "fit" anyone and is available with three different seat sizes and three different back heights. The Sensor chair also allows for easy maintenance with field-replaceable parts. The T- and loop-arms are interchangeable, or can be removed from the chair in the field. The pneumatic cylinder for height adjustment and the casters and glides can be replaced in minutes. Another excellent feature is that the upholstered one-piece seat and back cushion can be replaced on-site. The chair comes with a ten-year warranty and can be purchased at a very reasonable price, considering its quality.

Office panel systems include steel files; however, lateral or vertical files are usually purchased as freestanding items to be used singly or in groups in public areas, workrooms, or offices of the library. In addition to cabinets for paper storage, steel cases are also designed for other media—microfiche, microfilm, audio-cassettes, video-cassettes, computer printouts, and compact discs. Many poorly constructed files are on the market, but there is no reason to purchase files with drawers that do not operate smoothly, or with frames that bend easily when the cases are moved. High-quality files are available at reasonable prices from several reputable manufacturers, such as GF, Meridian, Steelcase, Storwal, and Sunar Houserman.

A 1982 article in *Library Technology Reports* (Buyers Laboratory, Inc.) reviews tests performed on lateral files. Drawers, doors, cabinets, and finishes

Figure 75. Krueger's Vertebra® chair. *Photograph courtesy of Krueger International.*

Figure 76. Herman Miller's Ergon 2™ chair. *Photograph courtesy of Herman Miller, Inc.*

Figure 77. The Equa® chair by Herman Miller. *Photograph courtesy of Herman Miller, Inc.*

Figure 78. Steelchase's ConCentrx chair. *Photograph courtesy of Steelcase, Inc.*

Figure 79. The Sensor chair by Steelcase. *Photograph courtesy of Steelcase, Inc.*

Figure 80. The Wilkhahn FS chair by Vecta. *Photograph courtesy of Vecta®.*

were tested in order to determine the following: stability of the files, quality of the hardware, ease of removing and replacing drawers and dividers, maximum extension of drawers, suspension, usable drawer space, thickness of the steel, and maintenance required. Although the particular files tested in 1982 may no longer be available, the information about the testing is still valid and can be used in selecting files today.

Lateral files are available in standard widths of 30″, 36″, and 42″. The height of the files varies from one manufacturer to another; however, most companies have files available in height ranges of 28″–30″, 40″–42″, 51″–53″, and 63″–65″. Lateral file cases come with two, three, four, and five drawers. Drawer heights differ from brand to brand, but several companies have standard drawer heights of 3″, 6″, 9″, 12″, and 15″. While the standard drawer depth for lateral files is 18″, one company, Meridian, has files available in both 18″ and 20″ depths.

The same companies that make lateral files also make vertical files which are available with two, three, four, and five drawers. The files are 15″ wide for letter-size and 18″ wide for legal-size filing. The drawers are 30″ deep. Vertical files come in heights of approximately 30″, 42″, 53″, and 60″. Both lateral and vertical files can be purchased with a variety of inserts for the interior, including dividers and trays for cards in sizes of 3″ × 5″, 4″ × 6″, and 5″ × 8″.

High-quality files have welded steel frames consisting of uprights and horizontal members under the outer steel cabinet. The better files have extra steel reinforcement at the stress points in the case. (See Figure 81). The case should be engineered in such a manner that the frame (and therefore the cabinet) will not bend when the file is moved, pushed, or placed on an uneven floor. (The drawers will not operate properly in a cheaply made file with a bent case.) The vendor should be able to supply evidence that the file has been performance-tested. Ask about warranty; Steelcase, for example, offers a ten-year warranty. Several companies offer five-year warranties. Other necessary features of lateral or vertical files include full-extension drawers riding on steel ball-bearing suspension, a safety interlock system to prevent the user from opening more than one drawer at a time, leveling glides, and counterweight packages.

Lateral and vertical files are also available as modular, stackable units. The advantage of these files is their flexibility. Additional modules can be added later, to be stacked on the initial installation. Also, it is easy for the consumer to design a file that will allow for storing a variety of media. One manufacturer that produces a high-quality system is Meridian. (See Figure 82). Both lateral and vertical

Figure 81. Six steel uprights and horizontal stretchers reinforce the frame of Steelcase files to prevent sway and to assure strength and squareness. *Photograph courtesy of Steelcase, Inc.*

files are available. The modules come in four heights, 11¾″, 13⅛″, 15⅛″, and 17⅛″. Half-height drawers are also available. Each module has its own inner frame with vertical and horizontal members for strength. The system includes open pass-through modules and planter tops. Unlike some other systems, high-pressure laminate tops with radius, as well as straight, edges are available. Another attractive feature added recently is the option of wood pulls on the drawers. This allows for coordinating the steel files with wood furnishings used in the same area.

While lateral and vertical files allow for the storage of multimedia, cases specifically designed to hold microforms and audio-visual materials are available. Steel storage cabinets purchased to hold these items should have the same heavy-duty construction as other high-quality files. Russ Bassett and Borroughs are two companies that make files to hold a variety of materials. Russ Bassett carries a full line of high-quality modular files that are specifically designed for microfiche, microfilm, and aperture cards. The cases also accommodate audio and video cassettes, and compact discs. The Russ Bassett products come with a ten-year warranty. (See Figure 83). Gaylord also sells a file for compact discs. As the popularity of discs increases, other suppliers of library furnishings will probably add similar files to their product lines.

Figure 82. Modular, stackable files made by Meridian. *Photograph courtesy of Meridian, Inc.*

Fully loaded files are as dangerous as fully loaded bookstacks. Before files are purchased, the librarian should provide the vendor with information as to how the files will be arranged, where they will be located in the building, and the kind of material that will be stored in them. Some files were not designed, for example, to hold the weight of microfiche or film. Also, how and where the files are placed determines how they will need to be anchored for stability. If they are placed in groups, several cases can be bolted together for strength. Single cases can be anchored to the floor or wall or a counterweight added to them for stability.

Once the information regarding use of the files has been provided, it is the job of the vendor and installer to make sure they can be used safely. Sometimes, when changes are made in a library, the original purpose of the files changes. As with steel bookstacks, it is a good idea to go back and check on the stability of files installed several years before. There should be no possibility that a case will fall over when a drawer is pulled out.

Several of the companies mentioned in this chapter sell tables and chairs for two other areas of the library not yet mentioned: the staff lounge and the community or meeting room. In the lounge,

tables with a metal leg or pedestal base and a high-pressure laminate top are often purchased for lunch tables. Berco, Krueger, Herman Miller, Redco, Steelcase, and many other contract furniture manufacturers sell tables appropriate for this use. Side chairs with a swivel base, like those made by Herman Miller and Steelcase, can be used in the lunchroom. Or the library can purchase metal-framed stacking chairs, such as those made by GF, Krueger, Steelcase, or Vecta, and use them in both the meeting room and the staff lounge. Another possibility is to use the Krueger nesting Matrix table and the Matrix stacking chair. The metal frames of both items can then be color-coordinated. (See Figures 84 and 85).

Stacking chairs can be purchased with caddies on which they are placed for moving and storage. Likewise, caddies are available to hold folding tables for the meeting room. Several companies make folding tables that look like any finely styled leg-base table. The problem with some of them, however, is that they are heavy and difficult to set up. If you are selecting a folding table that will have to be put up or down, or moved frequently, try out several tables being considered. Make sure that you choose one that is light and can be unfolded easily. In some

Figure 83. Russ Bassett makes steel storage cabinets with the heavy-duty construction needed to hold microforms and other media. *Photograph courtesy of Russ Bassett.*

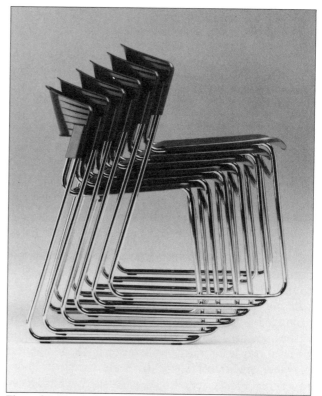

Figure 84. The Assisa stacking chair designed by Paolo Favaretto for Vecta. *Photography courtesy of Vecta®.*

situations, it might be best to select folding tables that are less stylish, but sturdy and lightweight, like Krueger's all-purpose tables with a honeycomb core construction in the top. Meeting room tables can be purchased in 24″ widths for classroom situations and larger widths for small meetings, children's activities, etc.

Figure 85. The Krueger Matrix® high-density stack chair and table. *Photograph courtesy of Krueger International.*

Chapter 9
Sign Systems and Display

Sign Systems

One of the most important, yet neglected, aspects of the library interior is the sign system. The emphasis here is on the word *system*. Even in a new building, the effect of good planning and design is destroyed when a library opens with signs in many shapes, colors, and styles. The lack of systematic signage also leads to a proliferation of hand-lettered or other makeshift signs. In their excellent book, *Designing Places for People*, authors C. M. Deasy and Thomas E. Lasswell note:

> The principal concern in designing libraries is the special aspect of cue searching called *wayfinding*. This is because so much of library use takes the form of a search for specific information or material. The searcher must quickly learn how to use the system in order to improve the chances of finding what is sought. (p. 107)

Many aspects of the building's design affect signage: the placement and kinds of lighting; finishes and colors selected for the building interior; architectural features such as soffits, concealed spline ceilings, stairways, halls, entrances, and exits; and the placement and styles of furniture. Planning of the sign system should take place along with the building design and the furniture selection.

The three factors considered when choosing furnishings—function, maintenance, and appearance—are also relevant to the selection of a sign system. Because signs play a vital role in public relations, their appearance is especially important. Inadequate, makeshift signage makes a poor impression on a public that is surrounded daily by effective systems in department stores, shopping malls, hospitals, and professional office buildings. Attractive signage demonstrates that the library is like a well-run company: the business is organized; planning has been done to see that the consumer finds needed goods and services easily; the interior has been designed to show that the organization is customer-responsive.

Just as the first step in a building project or the furniture selection process is the development of a program, the planning of a functional sign system begins with making decisions about what kinds of signs are needed and what they should accomplish. The system must include some of the following: (1) a directory or map near the entrance to identify locations for major departments or functions; (2) signs throughout the building to direct users to specific locations—up or down floors, around corners, and through halls or doors; (3) signs on doors or at the entrances to departments to identify the function or service within that room or area; (4) signs to provide information about regulations, warnings, procedures, instructions, and hours; (5) signs to highlight particular collections and services or to announce events taking place in the library; and (6) signs on the end panels of stacks to identify which books are shelved in that range.

A successful sign system is one that can be learned easily and is truly helpful to the user of the library. Here are some guidelines:

1. Consistency is essential to the development of an effective sign system. It allows the user to learn the system quickly and easily. Signs that serve the same function throughout the building, such as those giving instructions or those identifying specific departments, should have the same shape, size, layout, type size, and placement (height, location on the wall, etc.).
2. The sign system should be logical. Directions should be given in a progression from the general to the specific. Levels of information should be established so that some messages receive more emphasis than others.
3. Signs should use terminology consistently—only one term should be applied to any one area, service, etc. The words used should be as descriptive as possible and easily recognized by the public. Avoid using jargon that is familiar only to the staff.
4. Redundancy should be avoided. Too many signs, all providing the same message, can be as bad as no sign at all.

5. Signs should be placed appropriately at decision points in the building—at the entrance to the library, by elevators or stairs, at the end of a hall.

6. The text of a sign should be clearly and accurately written in order to communicate the intended message effectively. The phrases used and the length of the lines of text should be short, so the sign can be easily read and understood. The tone should be appropriate for promoting good public relations.

7. Signs should work well in relation to the architecture of the library. The dimensions of signs should be in proportion to the scale of the building. The colors and materials should coordinate with the colors and finishes of the building. Place signs where they will not be obscured by parts of the building, fixtures, or furnishings.

8. Signs should be made in accordance with the principles of good design. These principles pertain to typeface, size and spacing of letters and lines, contrast, use of symbols, and color. (Information about the effective design of signs can be found in a number of books. Some of them are listed in the bibliography at the back of this book.)

9. As the situation in the library changes, signs should be changed promptly to reflect the new conditions.

Three important maintenance aspects must be considered when selecting a sign system for a library. First, the system should be one that can be easily installed and has the flexibility to allow for frequent changes. Second, the system should remain attractive and useful for a long period of time, and should be constructed of materials that will not fade or wear out. Third, the system should be one that will be available in the future. If the signs are commercially produced, the manufacturer should be one who is likely to be in business for several years to come. If the signage is for a large building and involves a substantial investment, the service history of the product should be obtained and references to similar jobs should be checked. If the signs are to be produced in-house or by a small local supplier, the library should select materials that will be available for a number of years.

A workable sign system is dynamic, and allows a library to make changes frequently while still maintaining the integrity of the original design concept. Once a library has planned a sign system, the resulting information should be documented in the form of a sign manual, which will provide long-range guidance on signage for the organization. The manual should include guidelines and policies regarding the use of signs, placement and mounting, terminology, sizes, shapes, colors, design (typography, sym-

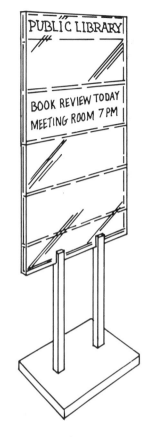

Figure 86. Freestanding, acrylic announcement boards are available from local manufacturers.

Figure 87. Directory boards are essential wayfinding devices. Shown here is a directory made by Modulex for Transylvania University, Lexington, Kentucky. *Photograph courtesy of Modulex.*

bols, spacing and size of letters and lines), construction, maintenance, and the use of temporary signs. Libraries seeking a model sign manual should read *A Sign System for Libraries* by Mary S. Mallery and Ralph E. DeVore (1982). That publication documents a system developed for the Western Maryland Public Libraries.

Just as with furnishings, some vendors will be glad to discuss signage for the library, make some suggestions as to possible systems, and provide specifications and pricing, even for small buildings. Because of the scope of the project and amount of detail involved, the development of a sign system for a large building should be done with the assistance of a sign consultant or a vendor with expertise in the area.

Signs that are considered permanent (identification of doors and major areas, directions to other floors, etc.) can be obtained from companies that supply a full range of products constructed of metal, wood, and plastic with letters applied by a variety of processes. Interior signs are also available from the major library suppliers such as Brodart, Demco, and Gaylord. Signs that require changing frequently, such as identification on the end panels of bookstacks or announcements of upcoming events, should either be replaced in-house or purchased from a local source that can supply new signs quickly and inexpensively.

A sign system may comprise several different kinds of signs. The Irving Public Library in Irving, Texas, for example, has a well-developed system of signs constructed from a variety of materials. Signage was not part of the architectural drawings, but was part of the work of the interior designer. The designer hired a consultant, who worked with the library director, Dr. Lamar Veatch, to plan the signs for the new central library that opened in 1986. The key element in the ongoing process of signmaking for the Irving library is a computerized signmaking machine for producing die-cut vinyl letters. The machine is used to make call numbers and subject headings for custom-designed plastic signholders on the end panels of the bookstacks. For identification and directional signs throughout the building, the letters are applied to acrylic panels or glass walls and doors. The signmaker is also used to cut letters for instructional signs and posters.

Major areas in the Irving library are identified by hanging signs ingeniously made for PVC (polyvinyl chloride) pipe. The ends of the pipe were filled in with discs of plexiglass. The pipe and ends were then painted to coordinate with the building interior. Vinyl letters were cut by the machine and applied to the pipe to create a finished sign. (See Figures 88 and 90).

Although the computerized signmaker is an expensive item, it should be considered for purchase by large libraries. The cost might be shared with

Figure 88. Hanging signs made from PVC pipe at Irving Public Library, Irving, Texas. *Photo: David J. Lund.*

Figure 89. Library areas can be identified with banners, as they are here at Morris Frank Branch, Houston Public Library. The banners are hung from a pipe-grid ceiling. *Photo: David J. Lund.*

another city department, another department of the university, or with a network of libraries. Life-cycle costing can be used to justify the expense. A public library with a main library and branches can use the machine to produce signs for all of its buildings. In Irving, large, inexpensive sheets of plexiglass are purchased and cut into smaller pieces; the machine is then used to produce the lettering for signs to be used in the branches as well as the main library.

Irving Public Library also has an interesting and helpful directory inside the main entrance. It is a personal computer placed attractively in a custom-built cabinet or kiosk. The software used is a customized version of a standard package designed for office building directories. The public uses the computer to access information about the location of materials and services in the building, and to read announcements of events taking place in the library.

Figure 90. Vinyl letters can be used on Plexiglas panels in many areas of the library. This custom end panel, built by Worden for Irving Public Library, has a plastic sign holder that can be removed when the vinyl letters need to be replaced. *Photo: David J. Lund.*

Several available modular sign systems are especially useful for libraries because they allow for ease in changing signs. One of the most flexible systems is manufactured by Modulex. The company offers a full line of permanent exterior and interior signs. The most interesting aspect of this system for libraries, however, is signage that uses the principle of the LEGO building-block toy. The system is an excellent solution to the problem of continually changing signs on the end panels of bookstacks. (See Figure 91). Aluminum frames are used to hold a plastic knob base. Letters, symbols, numbers, etc. are printed on LEGO-like pieces—one letter, symbol, or number on each piece. Users have an assortment of letters (pieces) which fit onto the knob base to create a line of text. Because the individual pieces fit together so

well, seams between individual letters (pieces) do not show on the finished line. The individual pieces provide correct alignment and spacing between letters. A finished line of text is locked in place. The changeable format can be used to create text on signs attached to walls, doors, or bookstacks, on hanging signs, and on many kinds of directory boards. The concept can also be used to make maps. Lines of the changeable type can be combined with modules of permanent silkscreened or vinyl die-cut text. Another attractive feature of the system is that panels with a baked enamel finish in bright colors are used with the lines of changeable type, to allow for coordinating the system with the color scheme of the building.

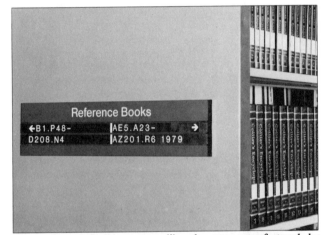

Figure 91. A flexible system like the one manufactured by Modulex allows for changing signs quickly and easily. *Photograph courtesy of Modulex.*

Another possibility for making small changeable signs, like those on the end panels of stacks, is a relatively inexpensive signmaking machine that produces pre-spaced and aligned vinyl letters that are attached to a self-adhesive strip. An example of this system is one made by Leteron. (This is actually a small, manual version of a signmaker like the one used at Irving.) The lines of text produced in-house can then be used on the modular sign panels of a system like Slatz, on plexiglass panels, or on other materials.

These are only a few approaches that can be taken to signage in the library. It is interesting to note that an increasing number of companies are exhibiting signs at conferences. The library supply catalogs are also now selling a wider variety than they have in the past. Signage is an area of interior planning that can benefit from new ideas. With encouragement, perhaps staff members will discover other ingenious, attractive, and inexpensive ways of constructing signs for the buildings in which they work.

Display

Librarians no longer sit quietly at their desks (if they ever did), as caretakers of a collection of the world's best books, waiting for someone to make a request for an item from the orderly shelves. In recent years, librarians have had to react to new kinds of materials, competition from other multimedia sources, an increasing number of informal educational organizations, and an aware public with access to a variety of leisure-time activities. Once again, libraries have looked to profit-making businesses to learn ways of taking a more aggressive approach to service. Librarians are seeking methods of drawing people into the library, where they are then offered a wide range of readily accessible materials and services. Materials are being merchandised to promote library use.

Merchandising of the library product involves continuous staff attention to the arrangement of the materials in the building, and to the manner in which the items are displayed. Patron use of some library materials depends to a great extent on how the materials are presented. Moreover, what works today to promote a product is not necessarily what will work tomorrow. Librarians who are skilled at promoting the use of their collections are aware of the value of change. Materials that are seldom used may be checked out more frequently if they are both moved to another location and displayed in another manner. Many libraries have taken a cue from bookstores, where lighted signs and display shelving are used to promote products. Upon entering the store, the customer encounters books and other products in displays. In a mall, the display even spills out into the corridor. The titles currently being promoted are changed frequently, and displays are moved around or rearranged regularly. In grocery and department stores, the same kind of merchandising techniques are used. Displays are found at the ends of aisles and at the entrances to departments. This method of promoting products takes advantage of the user's tendency to browse, and to pick up items that are within view and readily accessible.

Display furnishings should be treated as the most dynamic element in the library. They should allow for rearrangement of the materials displayed, as well as possible movement of all or part of the fixture itself. In Chapter 4, steel library shelving with display capabilities was mentioned. Bookstacks with shelves that have a backstop and are tipped up at an angle are now made by many companies. The shelves allow for displaying books face out; users can see book titles more easily on the angled shelves. Paperbacks can also be displayed on zigzag display units that are placed on regular library shelves that have been adjusted to tilt up. Display shelving is usually available with built-in sign boards and lights to draw the attention of the library user. Fixtures designed and sold to bookstores are another possibility for book display. Keep in mind, however, that you are not purchasing the same level of quality with these items that you are with library bookstacks. Such fixtures are not designed or built to last for the life of the library.

Paperback book racks are available in a wide variety of styles, with new models coming out all the time: double-faced and rotating wire racks, racks with rotating towers in wood and metal frames in many configurations, display units with bins for books, and modular wood and plastic units that can be reconfigured. Because the companies selling these items, such as Brodart, Demco, Gaylord, and Highsmith, add new products frequently, don't assume that an item purchased five years ago is still the best one for your situation. Furthermore, it may not be possible to buy a unit to match one that was purchased several years ago. Check the catalogs for new products and, if possible, look at what is new at conference exhibits. An interesting product, which can now be seen at conventions, is the Modul 'S' system manufactured by Gressco. (See Figure 92). The system consists of three basic units: the open box, the open cube, and a diagonal cube. The wooden units are held together by using a special plastic nut and bolt. The units can be configured in an unlimited number of ways to create islands and towers, as well as more imaginative "trains," "bridges," and "snakes." The modules can be used for storage and display of a browsing collection of books for adults or children.

Figure 92. Gressco's Modul 'S'™ system provides flexible storage and display for books and other materials. *Photograph courtesy of Gressco, Ltd.*

Many of the display systems available have units for audio-visual materials as well as books. Brodart, for example, sells a system of acrylic display shelving with units for paperback and hardback books, video cassettes, and records. The modules can be configured into freestanding units to use in the middle of the floor, or can be used against a wall or at the end of a range of bookstacks. All of the library supply companies have racks available for displaying video cassettes, audio cassettes, records, and compact discs. Some of these display racks are relatively expensive. If possible, take a look at those you are considering for purchase at conference exhibits or at another library. Make sure you are getting a sturdy piece of equipment, which will be stable when filled and will not fall apart when it is moved around the library. Some of the racks with rotating towers, for example, have no means for locking the towers in place. When the rack is moved, the towers have to be completely removed. If the towers fall off, the plastic parts break easily. Also, some of the display units are just not very attractive. Spend a little more money, if necessary, to purchase a rack that matches the decor of the library and the level of quality of the other furnishings. Another consideration when purchasing display furnishings is security. It is very time-consuming to keep audio-visual materials in a unit that is located in a reading area and has to be unlocked every time someone wants to check out an item. This is also a deterrent for users, who may not want to ask a staff member to get the material they want. Many libraries now opt for displaying the original container for the cassette or disc in the public area, while keeping the actual item in a storage unit behind the desk. Users bring the original box to the desk and exchange it for the material as they check it out.

One of the most versatile multimedia display systems is Frameworks, available from Gaylord. (See Figure 93). Books, magazines, records, compact discs, and audio and video cassettes can be displayed. The modular system consists of wooden "slatwalls" and wire "gridwalls," from which can be hung a variety of units, including sloping shelves, display bins, wire racks, and individual angled

holders. Rotating paperback, audio- and video-cassette, and compact-disc racks can be placed in wood frame units that are part of the system. Fabric-covered, Velcro tack-board modules are also available. One of the advantages of a multimedia unit like Frameworks is that it can be used to display community notices and giveaway items, as well as library materials. Because of the increasing interest in merchandising library materials, other companies are likely to develop similar multimedia display systems.

Figure 93. Frameworks, made by Gaylord, is a versatile, multimedia display system. *Photograph courtesy of Gaylord Bros., Syracuse, N.Y.*

Chapter 10
The Bid Process

When a large amount of public money is to be used for the purchase of library furnishings, a formal bid process is usually employed to award the contract. A competitive bid situation allows the purchaser to analyze and judge comparable products for a particular project on the basis of quality and cost. Over a period of time, as a number of contracts are awarded, the bid process ensures the distribution of public funds among a number of suppliers. Unfortunately, the buying process involves many variables, and a number of problems inherent to the process make bidding difficult for both the purchaser and the vendor. This is especially true of a project that involves large sums of money and requires a full set of detailed specifications.

The Bid Package

The preparation of a bid package requires expertise in the writing of specifications and knowledge of the elements of the bid document. Care must be taken to ensure that the package covers a wide range of contingencies. Even when the documents are well-written, they are subject to misinterpretation by the bidders. Subjective judgment is often involved in qualifying bidders, approving alternates, and awarding the bid. Although the bid process is planned to be fair to all involved, it allows for manipulation by both suppliers and purchasers. The best that can be hoped for is that all parties involved will act with integrity and understand their responsibilities in the process. (This will be discussed in Chapter 11.)

The written programming done at the beginning of the selection process (as outlined in Chapter 2) becomes valuable when making actual purchases. Furniture selections made on the basis of a particular level of quality can now be defended with authority, *provided all parties involved in awarding the bid have been educated throughout the process.* It is a critical error for a librarian to select particular furnishings and put them out for bid without involving all of the decision makers in the process. If a purchasing agent or any other person involved in the

process does not truly understand the level of quality needed, poor-quality items may be purchased because a low bid is awarded as a matter of course. Architects, designers and consultants, purchasing agents, library boards, friends of the library, college or university administrators, school boards, members of the city council, the city administrator, etc.—any of these groups or individuals may play a vital role in awarding the bid. It is the librarian's responsibility to see that key people understand why a particular level of quality is necessary, and what products can provide this level. One of the points to make in educating those involved is that high-quality furniture is apt to be higher in price than furniture of a lower quality, but the latter will not hold up with heavy library use. It is easier to justify furniture selections prior to the purchasing process than to explain why a low bid is not acceptable when the decision makers have the bids in front of them and are able to compare dollars. Your best ally is a purchasing agent or representative who knows the value of using sound judgment in awarding a bid, and who has the confidence to stand behind a decision based on factual evidence.

A complete bid package consists of two parts: (1) documents detailing the requirements for bidding and successful completion of the contract, and (2) specifications for the particular items of furniture to be purchased. While the librarian will be involved in developing the bid package, the document that provides the legal basis for the contract will, of course, be reviewed by an attorney.

The bid process should include a pre-bid conference to be held approximately one week after the package goes out for bid. Potential bidders are encouraged to attend the conference in order to ask for clarification of the bid process and document, and to ask questions they may have about the specifications of the particular items included. The purchasing agent, the librarian, and any other parties directly involved with awarding the bid will be in attendance to review the documents with the bidders, answer questions, and make note of items that may require an addenda to the original bid package.

A complete sample bid document can be found in *The Procurement of Library Furnishings, Specifications, Bid Documents, and Evaluation* (Poole and Trezza). The book contains the proceedings of a Library Equipment Institute conducted in 1966. Even though the book was published over twenty years ago, the information is still relevant.

Bid documents customarily include the sections discussed in this chapter. Not all bid packages require every section, and it is more important that essential items be covered somewhere in the document than that they are included in a specific section. The quotations from bid packages are included in order to provide readers with examples of how the documents *might* be worded; there are many ways to state the stipulations of the bid and the specifications. In some cases, the examples do not apply to the usual bid situation, but are provided to illustrate how a number of contingencies can be covered in a bid document in an unusual situation

Invitation to Bid: This section gives notice of what will be purchased and includes details of when and where bids will be accepted. Information may also be given regarding the withdrawal of bids and any bonds required for bidding.

Instructions to Bidders: The legal aspects of the bidding procedure are covered here, including damages to be incurred by the contractor for failure to execute the contract on time, details on how bids are to be submitted, a bid-bond form, and statements about the owner's right to request samples and to require performance testing. This section should have a paragraph noting the right of the owner to accept or reject any or all bids, and to reject bids submitted with irregularities or qualifications. The instructions also include procedures for the bid and award of particular sections of the package. For example:

> Bidders must bid on each and every item in any section for which a bid is submitted. Bids will be considered only by complete sections; partial section bids will be regarded as "no bids" on the particular section involved.

Or:

> Awards may be made by line item, by section, or on an "all or none" basis.

One of the most important statements in this section establishes the owner's right to gather evidence of the bidders' qualifications, and to reject the bids of those who cannot prove their ability to complete the project successfully:

> The owner reserves the right to visit the factory of the manufacturer of the furniture offered in this bid in order to determine the capability of the company to produce furniture in the quantities required. The owner also reserves the right to make inquiries to determine the financial condition of bidders. The bidder must be in a financial position to obtain all materials, services, and labor to carry out the obligations of the contract. In no case will a purchase order be issued until the owner is completely satisfied of the bidder's professional craftsmanship, financial condition, and manufacturing capability.

It is essential that bidders be informed of the factors that will be considered in awarding the bid, and that they understand that the contract will be granted to the lowest *responsible* bidder:

> The owner will award the contract to the lowest and most responsible bidder who submits the most advantageous bid to the owner. In determining the most advantageous proposal, the following factors will be considered: conformity to specifications, delivery capabilities, purchase price, life expectancy of items bid, cost of maintenance, product warranty, and past performance in similar projects.

Or:

> The owner reserves the right to reject any or all bids and is not bound to accept the lowest bid submitted. If the lowest bid is not the best bid of value received for monies expended in the owner's opinion, the right is reserved to make awards in the best interests of the owner. In making awards, intangible factors such as bidder's service, integrity, reputation, and past performance will be weighed, as well as tangible evidence of equipment quality and aesthetic appeal.

Many times, specific manufacturers are referenced in the detailed specifications. In the instructions to bidders, a statement should be made that brand names are given in order to establish a level of quality. This information can be combined with instructions for obtaining "approved equal" status where the detailed specifications use this terminology. The bid document should identify clearly who will have the responsibility for determining equal status. (Sometimes this information is given in the General Conditions section, rather than in Instructions to Bidders.)

> It is not the intent of the specifications, drawings, or schedules to limit the materials or items to be procured by these documents to the product of any particular manufacturer, distributor, or supplier. Where any article, item, material, or thing is specified by a proprietary name, trade name, manufacturer, catalog number, or any other identification, it has been done so as to set a definite standard and/or style and to provide a reference for comparison as to quality, design, appearance, physical conformity and approximate dimensions, and other required characteristics, including equivalent value. It is not the intention to discriminate against or prevent any manufacturer, distributor, or supplier from furnishing an "approved equal" product, subject to the approval of the owner as to the equality thereof, which

meets or exceeds all the characteristics of the item specified.

It is distinctly understood (1) that the library consultant will use his or her judgment in determining whether or not any article or thing proposed to be substituted is the equal of any article specified; (2) that the decision of the consultant on all such questions of equality shall be final; and (3) that in the event of any adverse decision by the consultant, no claim of any sort will be made or allowed against the consultant or the owner.

Actual samples of items bid as "approved equals" shall be submitted, with catalog illustrations. Manufacturers' specifications, either written on their letterhead or printed in their literature, must accompany such items. Those items submitted for prior approval, and which are then approved, will be listed in addenda to the specifications and will be bound with the contract document. Submission of items for prior approval must be made not later than twenty-one (21) calendar days prior to date of bid opening.

The instructions to bidders may also include a statement about the owner's right to increase or decrease quantities slightly (usually no more than 10%) and procedures for bidding any add alternates that are part of the package. (Add alternates are items that the library would like to purchase, if funds are available. These items are usually presented as a group in the bid package, with the library retaining the the right to purchase all or any of the items in the quantity noted or fewer.) The actual schedule of items to be purchased and forms for submitting unit prices and total amounts may be in this section or may be included with the detailed specifications.

General Conditions: This section should cover information that relates more specifically to this job. (It is difficult, however, to see why some items are usually included here rather than elsewhere in the document!) This section includes statements covering the following: contractor's obligations to furnish materials and labor for installation, the owner's right to inspect items furnished, requirements for the contractor to replace rejected or damaged pieces, penalties paid by the contractor in the event of delays or failure to fulfill the contract, acceptance of work completed, guarantees, and a referral to floor plans attached to the document. The General Conditions section also outlines the contractor's obligation to make field measurements of the building:

It is the successful contractor's responsibility to obtain and verify all field measurements to assure proper installation of all work. No additional costs shall be charged to the owner for modification of library custom wood furniture required to provide proper installation.

A project involving a new building or major renovation often presents problems in regard to delivery. The problem lies as much with the difficulty of predicting when a building will be completed as it does with the availability of the furniture. It is very difficult to time the purchasing of furnishings so precisely that the factory can schedule production and deliver the items as soon as the building is completed. While bid documents include penalties for the late delivery by a vendor, no provisions are made, unfortunately, for the charges incurred by a contractor who can supply items on time, but is forced to accommodate delays in the completion of a building. Sometimes the scheduling of delivery can be complicated (as in the example given here); the details need to be included in the bid document in order to avoid misunderstandings:

Delivery and installation of furniture to be provided in this contract shall be performed in two (2) phases which will coincide with the completion of phases of the general construction contract. The two phases are as follows: PHASE I - Completion of the first and second level additions to the library building; PHASE II - Completion of the interior renovation of the existing library building. Completion of the general construction contracts for each phase, for the purposes of this furniture contract, shall occur after all final inspections are approved and the issuance of an occupancy permit by the city.

All furniture included in Phase I (as represented by drawings F-2 and F-3) must be delivered, installed in place, and clean within a period of ten (10) calendar days immediately following the general construction contract completion of Phase I. All furniture included in Phase II (as represented by drawing F-1) must be delivered, installed in place, and clean within a period of ten (10) calendar days immediately following the general construction contract completion of Phase II.

Completion dates of the general construction work in each phase as projected at this date are as follows: Completion of Phase I - June 1, 1991; Completion of Phase II - August 15, 1991. The general construction completion dates will be revised as work progresses in the general construction. The Contractor should, however, be prepared to furnish all items for Phase I any time between June 1, 1991 and September 1, 1991. In like manner, the Contractor should be prepared to furnish all items for Phase II any time between August 15, 1991 and November 15, 1991. The Architect reserves the right to adjust these "delivery windows" in the event of unusual, unforeseen events. In an effort to minimize problems with delivery of furniture and conflicts with this contract, the Architect shall issue written updated completion schedules to the successful Contractor(s) during the first week of each month.

The Contractor shall be responsible for all coordination of the delivery of furniture to be provided as required, to coincide with the completion of each phase of the general construction contract. No furniture shall be delivered and stored on the site prior to its installation. The Contractor shall be responsible for any and all storage of furniture prior to delivery and installation.

Requirements regarding where, when, and how deliveries are to be made are also covered in the General Conditions, along with statements about protecting the building during installation, clean-up required, and final acceptance of the furnishings:

All deliveries shall be made during regular business hours. Contractor or his representative shall be at the job site to accept all deliveries. No drop-shipping shall be allowed. Under no circumstances will the owner be obligated to receive deliveries. The Contractor shall be required to provide protective runways (plastic or other suitable material) on all finished floors throughout the building in areas where furniture is being transported or installed. All furniture will be initially delivered at the loading dock on the north side of the building. Furniture delivered for Phase I shall enter the new addition through the Receiving Room, No. 120. (See Drawing F-2) Furniture delivered for Phase II shall enter the existing building through the Theatre, No. 106. (See Drawing F-1).

The bid document should also spell out terms of payment of the contract:

For the satisfactory fulfillment of the order for furniture, payment in full shall be due as stated below: First - 85% of the value of the material and items on the premises, when substantially all of it has been delivered and installed or placed in storage awaiting installation. Second - The balance of the order sum within 30 days after acceptance of all installed items.

Either the General Conditions section or the detailed specifications must include a statement about the submission of shop drawings by the successful contractor, and details concerning the approval of the drawings. Shop drawings should be required for any items that are custom-designed or are modifications of a standard item. The dimensions and construction of items illustrated on the shop drawings should be examined by the architect, the designer or consultant, and the librarian.

Standard Forms and Agreements: The legal agreement for the contract between the owner and supplier are given here, along with other necessary forms.

Miscellaneous Items: This section will include wage scales, taxes and other charges, patents and licenses, required insurance, etc.

Detailed Specifications by Bid Group: Furnishings are usually grouped in such a manner that vendors who supply certain kinds of items can bid all of one group and as many groups as they wish. Library bids may include the following groups: steel bookstacks, wood technical furniture and bookstacks, standard contract office furniture, and upholstered items, including chairs and sofas. Sometimes, the chairs are included with the technical furniture.

The specifications may include details regarding the mandatory submission of samples. Because the provision of samples is expensive for the manufacturer, the practice of requiring them tends to discourage bidders who really are not qualified to handle the level of quality and magnitude of some projects. Sometimes, samples are required prior to the bid process, and are used as part of the process of pre-qualifying bidders.

Bidders can be pre-qualified either by the submission of samples or by receiving "approved equal" status for their products as noted earlier. The results of the pre-qualification process are published as an addenda to the original bid documents. Pre-qualification lengthens the time needed to complete the bid process. The timing of the bid might be something like this: the package is put out for bid with an announcement of a pre-bid conference to be held a week later; the bidders are given three weeks following the conference to submit samples; the library requires two weeks prior to the day of the bid opening to review the samples and mail out addenda with the results of the pre-qualification. The process, therefore, requires at least six weeks.

Only the bids submitted by those companies approved as qualified prior to the bid opening should be considered legitimate bids. Do not require samples if you are not prepared to follow the stipulations of the bid exactly. It is an abuse of the bid process, and is unfair to reliable manufacturers, when an owner waives the requirement for a sample, or extends the submission deadline, because some company that was expected to bid did not provide the sample in time. Failure to submit the sample according to the bid document should automatically disqualify that company as a bidder. Furthermore, do not request samples if they really aren't needed, or if the decision makers are not absolutely sure of the level of quality and style desired. It is a waste of everyone's time and money if a sample for a particular item is requested, and the purchaser then decides that the library didn't really need that quality or want that style after all. Here is a sample statement for requiring samples prior to the bid opening:

To ensure that the specified products are furnished and installed in accordance with the design intent and the level of quality desired, procedures have been established for advance submittal of sample for review and approval by the Owner prior to receipt of bids. All samples shall be of the exact design, size, construction, material, detail and finish of the products proposed to be furnished in this Contract. The samples received shall be inspected and reviewed by the Owner to determine each Contractor's acceptability to bid on the Contract. All determinations shall be based on the initial samples submitted; Contractors shall not be permitted to resubmit samples if the initial samples are rejected. Decisions by the Owner shall be final.

The samples, when approved, shall be used as the basis of the minimum acceptable quality of all similar furniture to be supplied by the successful Contractor. Any and all subsequent furniture delivered to the job site that does not meet the quality of the approved samples shall be rejected and removed by the Contractor.

Samples must be received in the office of the Architect at least fourteen (14) days prior to the opening of bids. Contractor is responsible for any unpacking, set-up, or installation of samples necessary for complete review in the office of the architect. Each Contractor submitting samples shall be notified in writing by the Owner of approval or rejection of the items submitted. Only those Contractors who are approved shall be permitted to submit a bid for this Contract.

Submit one complete sample of all of the following items: 1) Item W-21, adult reading chair; 2) Item W-14, adult lounge chair; 3) Item W-8, catalog and computer table, including complete operable electrical system. Contractor must demonstrate, to the satisfaction of the Owner, evidence of an understanding of and compliance with the electrical requirements of this project, by providing literature or documented statements of the same information. Evidence of completed projects including this type of electrical requirement will suffice for meeting this criteria, also. 4) Item S-5, one (1) double-faced section of steel shelving, 66″ high × 24″ deep with one 24″-deep closed-base shelf, and eight adjustable 10″-deep shelves with one end panel and a canopy top.

Samples shall remain the property of the submitting Contractor. All arrangements and charges associated with the shipping and handling of submitted samples shall be the responsibility of each Contractor. All samples shall be removed from the Architect's office within seven (7) days after receipt of written notice to do so. Samples submitted by the successful Contractor shall be retained to be incorporated into the project at the appropriate time.

Samples are sometimes requested from the successful bidder following the award of the contract in order to ensure that the furnishings will be built according to exact specifications and with the level of quality desired. Here again, the owner retains the sample to use as a model against which the quality of the rest of the shipment can be measured.

The specific qualifications of bidders are set out in this part of the bid document. Usually, manufacturers must have produced items of the type specified for at least five years, and be able to provide the names of at least three installations of equal or larger size that they have done in the last five years. The bidder can also be required to provide evidence that the furniture in the referenced projects was actually made in the company's manufacturing plant, or in a factory where the company had responsibility for controlling the quality of the products. If there is any question about the qualifications of a bidder or the ability of the manufacturer to supply the item as specified (especially in a large project), the librarian and/or others involved in the project should tour the factory and visit some of the referenced projects.

The introduction to the detailed specifications for each group of furnishings may include background information about the project, requirements for style or design, materials, workmanship, testing, samples of finishes, cleanup, and guarantees. Detailed specifications can be written in several ways. Standard contract office furniture can usually be specified simply by stating the relevant order information:

> Desk chair, type II, mid-back, armless, overall height: 33½″ to 38½″; overall width: 20½″; seat height: 16″ to 21″, pneumatic height control, dual wheel casters, upholstered in Pointille, grey value 4, #F264; outer shell, base, and casters in #6205 black. (Steelcase Sensor chair #458-1203)

Guarantees and performance specifications can also be included, if the purchaser wants to ensure a particular level of quality.

Performance specifications are sometimes used. Unfortunately, many products have not been performance-tested, so it is difficult to describe what is needed in these terms. Also, performance specs do not allow for meeting the needs of the library in terms of design. There are performance specs for steel bookstacks, standard tests for wood finishes, and, as discussed in Chapters 7 and 8, some performance specifications for tables and chairs.

Most specifications are detailed descriptions of the materials and construction to be used in manufacturing an item. Performance specifications can be included with the description. An individual specification will include the kind of item; the dimensions; finishes and upholstery; electrical requirements; type of wood construction (three-ply particleboard, five-ply lumber core, etc.); joinery to be used; hardware; special features or modifications required in construction; and the name of a vendor to establish the level of quality. If the furniture of more than one manufacturer is acceptable from the standpoint of style and construction, include the names and model numbers for several products. Do not include special features of an item unless they are necessary. If you will accept a product that does not have the feature, do not mention it in the specifications. An example of a detailed specification for a table with custom features and a standard library chair with a slight modification would read thus:

Catalog and computer table. 68″ wide × 74⅞″ long × 42″ high. Double-faced with electrical system and four-compartment call slip units. (Stand up reference table)

Table top will be constructed of five-ply lumber core, 1¼″ thick with a .050″ high-pressure laminate face. The two sides will be edged with a 2″ × 2″ band of solid oak, shaped to a 1⅜″ radius, splined and glued to the lumber core and flush with the laminate. Panel ends will be constructed of 1⁷⁄₁₆″ five-ply lumber core with select oak veneer on the face and back. The panel will be edged with a 4″ wide band of solid oak, splined flush to all four sides of the core. The band will be shaped to a 1½″ radius on the top two corners and a ½″ radius on the bottom two corners. All four corners will be mitered and double-doweled. The edges of the oak band will have a continuous bullnose shape. The panels will have a double-rout detail. The first rout will be 2½″ from the edge of the panel and will be ¼″ × ¼″. The second rout will be ½″ from the interior edge of the first rout and will be ³⁄₁₆″ × ³⁄₁₆″. Both routs will be curved to match the radiused edges on all four corners of the panel. Each panel end will be equipped with a pair of adjustable leveling glides. The table will have a longitudinal stabilizing keel 1″ thick × 8″ wide, five-ply lumber core construction with select oak face and back. Bottom edge shall be banded with ⅛″ solid oak and machined to receive a steel bracket. The keel shall be attached to the underside of the top by means of ¾″ square screw cleats and at the bottom by means of ⁵⁄₁₆ × ¾ black oxidized truss head machine screw passing through a bracket into Rosans embedded in the end panel. Each side of the table will be equipped with a three-compartment call slip unit. The assembled unit will have all edges rounded, then finished to match the table. The finished unit will be positioned at the center of each table edge and screwed to the underside of the table top. The interior dimensions of each compartment will be 3½″ high × 3½″ wide × 5″ deep. The table will be equipped with an electrical raceway mounted flush with the writing surface and located in the center of the table along the full length of the top. See specifications above for Electrical System. Laminate: Formica, Storm, #912. (Worden X-2800 series modified)

Adult reading chair. 19¼″ wide × 19½″ deep × 32″ high. Seat height 18″. Back height 12″. Modified armless sled-base side chair.

Front legs will be solid oak 1³⁄₁₆″ × 2½″ with all edges and bottom shaped to a 1⅞″ radius coped and double-doweled into the side rail and sled rails. Sled-base runners shall be constructed of 1³⁄₁₆″ × 2½″ members. Runners will be set flush to bottom of front and back leg and will be double-doweled and glued in place. All bottom corners of leg and runners will be radiused to a minimum ³⁄₁₆″ radius corner. The side seat rail will be solid oak 1³⁄₁₆″ × 2½″ coped and double-doweled into the front leg and back post and

have radiused edges. The back seat rail shall be 1³⁄₁₆″ × 2½″ solid oak, double-doweled into the back posts. The front rail shall be 1³⁄₁₆″ × 3″ solid oak, double-doweled and glued to the front and back posts. The cross stretchers shall be 1″ × 1⅜″ solid oak, double-doweled into the front and back posts. Corner blocks shall be used to reinforce the rail to the leg and rail-to-back-post attachment. These shall be glued and screwed to the frame rails with two (2) 1¼″ - #10 screws. The seat will have a hardwood frame doweled and glued and sprung, using 9 gauge and 12 gauge calibrated sinuous springs. A ½″ fabric backed polyurethane foam shall be applied to the frame, then covered with 1¼″-thick fire-retardant polyurethane foam with 2.2 lbs. density and 55 lbs. ILD. The front edge will be radiused and upholstered. All seams will be double-stitched. The seat will be attached to the front and back rails with wood screws. The chair will have a fully upholstered back constructed on a 1¼″-thick hardwood frame, webbed with Propex and covered front and back with 1″-thick fire-retardant polyurethane foam with 1.2 lbs. density and 32 lbs. ILD. The back frame assembly will be covered with upholstery. The bottom edge of the back frame will be grooved to receive the fabric and upholstery fasteners in a neat and secure manner. The back frame will be secured to the back posts by means of four antique bronze hex drive connector bolts through the back posts into inserts in the internal back frame assembly. The back of the chair will be modified with an arch that will be coordinated with the curve used on the back of the lounge furniture and the children's reading chair. Back will be curved so that it will be approximately 2″ higher at the top of the radius than at either side. Upholstery: Arc Com Pentagon #61421, Blossom #2, 50% nylon, 50% rayon, 100% cotton back. (Worden X-C1106-USB 12 modified)

In addition to the specification for each item, general paragraphs should cover the requirements for wood and other materials, standard construction, and finishing processes. Specifications for steel bookstacks will include a list of the individual items needed by size, as well as a general section describing the construction, material, and finish of the shelving. The manufacturer or vendor will supply these specifications.

Specification writing requires specialized knowledge and expertise. Most vendors and manufacturers will provide detailed specifications for their products. Designers and library consultants who are hired to plan the interior of the library will write the specifications as part of their job. Specifications are also written by members of architectural firms, purchasing agents, or facilities managers.

The award of bids for furniture is seldom a simple matter of accepting the low bids. Usually, a number of factors have to be studied in making the purchasing decisions. The more specific and clearly written the bid requirements are, the easier it is to decide which suppliers will receive the contracts. If the low bid deviates from the bid documents or does not meet the specifications in regard to style or level of quality, or if the bidder cannot meet the delivery date or has not supplied required samples, the bid should not be considered "responsible." If informa- tion regarding the qualifications of the manufacturer cannot be obtained, the bid should be rejected. Like- wise, the burden of demonstrating that an alter- native item is an equal lies with the bidder, not with the purchaser. The bid process works only if all parties act responsibly. These responsibilities are dis- cussed in Chapter 11.

Chapter 11
The Library Furniture Market

The bid process as discussed in Chapter 10 should be advantageous for both the purchaser and the supplier, the two parties involved in the market transaction. The market can benefit both the library buying the furnishings and the company selling the products, if both parties accept and carry out their responsibilities in the selection and purchase process.

Furnishings are but one part of the total environment that makes a library work. For this reason, the selection of furniture involves a number of factors that lie outside the scope of the bid process itself. Because of the many considerations that enter into selection decisions, most librarians and others involved in a project know what products they want to buy when furniture goes out for formal bid or when prices are negotiated on an informal basis. These considerations include questions such as: Will the style of the furniture coordinate with the architecture of the building? Has the organization used a particular manufacturer before and found its products to be satisfactory in a similar situation? Do the new furnishings have to match existing items? Has the library found over the years that service is better from one company than from another?

In making purchases, the buyer does her/his part by selecting furniture according to the process discussed in Chapters 1 through 9. The librarian begins by developing a furniture program that outlines what is desired in terms of function, maintenance, and appearance. Then s/he, in conjunction with the others involved in the purchase, researches the available products. The librarian talks to vendors in the area and visits the relevant booths at conferences. (It won't take long for word to get around to the suppliers that there's a library in the market for furniture.) Any vendor who may want to bid is given an opportunity to discuss the project and explain why her/his products will be best for the library. The librarian asks lots of questions and evaluates how well the particular furnishings of each manufacturer will fill the needs of the library. S/he takes the time to educate and inform the other parties who will play a key role in awarding the bid. The others may also read this book, talk to manufacturers and dealers, or visit a factory. The investigation of products continues until the decision makers feel certain that they will be able to stand behind their choices when the bids come in, and to objectively justify the purchases.

The bid process differs, depending on the situation. In some cases, the library may want to reference more than one product as acceptable for particular items of furniture. The librarian may feel that any one of two or three different products will work for the library. This is likely to be the case where the furniture to be purchased will be a standard library chair to be used with a manufacturer's standard leg-base table and technical furniture. It is also possible to list only one product for some items and reference several brands on another item. For example, if the library will find either a Storwal or Steelcase file acceptable, both can be listed. Likewise, the library might note that two-position chairs made by Adden, Buckstaff, or Worden are acceptable. On the other hand, the library may decide that Brodart's metal leg reading table will coordinate best with the building, so it may be the only table referenced. (While you don't have to have one manufacturer make everything, it is wise to remember that splitting a package among several manufacturers on a small project may mean you will not get the best price from any one of them.)

In some situations, there may be only one manufacturer who makes the item you want. That does not mean you cannot buy it. If this were the case, we would never see any new products on the market. You may have a new building with a high-tech style that demands a particular design of furniture. You can, for example, specify and justify the purchase of Worden's Diametron tables and chairs, even though there are no other products like them available at the time of the bid. Likewise, if you have a large budget, you may specify custom furniture that very few manufacturers have the capability of producing.

Librarians can benefit from knowing how furniture is sold. Different manufacturers of library and contract furniture sell their products in different ways.

Some manufacturers will submit a direct bid from the factory. Some products are "open lines" and can be sold by any dealer. (Dealers are companies that handle the products of many different manufacturers.) Some items are sold by a limited number of dealers "authorized" by the factory to sell in a given area. Other manufacturers have "exclusive" dealers who are the only ones allowed to sell the product within a particular geographical area. Some large companies, like Steelcase, have representatives, showrooms, or regional managers who coordinate the market in a particular area and provide information and pricing to authorized dealers, but do not themselves generate orders or submit bids.

Most library manufacturers have representatives ("reps") who handle the market in a specific geographical area. The rep acts as a liaison between customers and the factory, or between dealers and the factory, by answering questions and providing information about the product, providing pricing to dealers, placing orders, and sometimes, providing additional services to customers such as space planning or the writing of specifications. In a bid situation, the rep may bid the furniture her/himself or supply pricing to dealers who bid.

When a decision is made as to which products will be the best for a particular situation, the librarian notifies the appropriate vendors of the items selected, usually a supplier of wood library furniture and, if appropriate, a supplier of steel shelving. The companies are informed that the library is interested in their product, and would like to work with them on developing specifications.

What is happening when a vendor agrees to work with you on a project? Salespeople in the library business have the knowledge and expertise to assist with space planning, preparation of a bid document, and the writing of specifications. Some of them will say that they are doing this for you for free; however, it is important to remember that these companies *are* in business. It is reasonable to expect that somewhere along the line, someone is going to pay for the work. It may be built into the prices of the items bid on the project, or your neighbor library may pay in its project, or you may pay the next time you go to the same supplier for something else. It's all right to take advantage of this service, but understand that it *is* being paid for.

You can get assistance another way—by hiring a library consultant who specializes in doing interiors. An interiors consultant has the library experience to understand what functional considerations are important in selecting furniture, and the knowledge of furniture necessary to select the best product for a situation. If there is also an interior designer involved in the project, the library consultant acts as a liaison between the staff and the designer or architect. While the designer will know about furniture generally, the consultant will be better informed about library products specifically. The consultant will be familiar with the manufacturers and vendors of library furniture, will have visited the major factories, and will know what's happening in the industry. S/he will know the capability of the manufacturers, the kinds of materials they typically use, and their standard construction techniques. Consultants are aware that there are many different ways to furnish a library and many different products available; some are appropriate in one situation, and some in another. The interiors consultant is not bound, like a salesperson, to specify only the products of particular manufacturers. The library hiring a consultant receives information about a wide range of products, and has an opportunity to purchase the best quality available for the money. The funds spent for a consultant are, it is true, not hidden. Because of the specialized knowledge that person brings to the job, however, the library hiring a consultant will very likely receive more quality for its money and will be assured of furnishing the building at or below budget. Because of the time and expertise needed, a consultant can be as helpful on a small project as on a large one. The library can be assured that the interior will be distinctive, functional, and attractive, even though there are not many dollars to spend nor many square feet to furnish.

The best interests of both librarians and those in the library furniture business are served if all parties act honestly and responsibly in the purchase process. Actions that are unfair to either the buyer or the seller are a detriment to the industry, and result in higher prices and, possibly, lower overall quality. It is very frustrating for everyone who understands the role of the parties in the market—both librarians and those in the industry—when individuals and organizations do not act responsibly.

Supplier Responsibilities

The relationship between supplier and purchaser imposes certain responsibilities on each side. The responsibilities of the supplier include the following:

1. The vendor should be knowledgeable about the product lines represented and be able to provide information about standard products, basic construction and materials, the capability of the manufacturer to do custom work, the limitations of the factory, special features of the products, and where and how the items can best be used. The salesperson should be able to discuss the positive aspects of her/his product without making unfounded negative comments about the work of competitors.

2. Once the decision has been made as to what products best fit the needs of the library, the vendor should supply budget pricing and speci-

fications upon request. In some cases, the vendor may also assist with space planning.

3. The vendor should understand the purchase process and be reliable in following the procedures exactly as they are stipulated in the bid document. S/he should attend the pre-bid conference. Having accepted the terms of the bid and asked all relevant questions in regard to approved items, equivalents, etc., prior to submitting a bid, the vendor should accept the decision of the purchaser, if all of the terms of the bid document have been carried out in the selection process.

4. A vendor who has been awarded a contract should provide the purchaser with regular updates in regard to the delivery date, discuss any problems or questions that arise in the production of the items, and work cooperatively with the purchaser to accommodate changes in schedule on the part of either party. The vendor is obligated to supply the items as specified and bid, unless a change has been agreed upon by both parties.

5. It is the responsibility of the vendor to see that the items are correctly and expeditiously installed, whether s/he supervises the installation on site or subcontracts the work to another company. If the vendor subcontracts the job, the scope and details of the work should be carefully reviewed with the subcontractor prior to the installation. Likewise, the installer should have all relevant shop drawings and specifications as well as the knowledge and expertise to interpret the documents. The supplier should provide any special instructions needed for the use or maintenance of the products. If parts are missing, or items are not received or are incorrectly supplied, the installer should notify the vendor, who should then take action immediately to work out a solution to the problem and correct the mistake.

6. The vendor should follow up on all questions that appear at the time of the installation and correct any problems that are the result of faulty workmanship, materials, etc. The most reliable suppliers will work cooperatively to correct problems even after the warranty period, if it is obvious that the manufacturer was at fault.

7. Manufacturers have an obligation to be customer-responsive. They should know how libraries function, attempt to develop new products or improve old ones to meet the needs of the library, and maintain quality control of their products.

Purchaser Responsibilities

The purchaser also has a set of responsibilities. In order to keep prices reasonable and keep the market competitive, it is as important for the librarian to act responsibly in the selection and purchase process as it is for the supplier. This side of the transaction is, unfortunately for our profession, sometimes ignored:

1. It is the responsibility of the librarian or other purchasing agent to gather information and make selection decisions based on knowledge and understanding of the products available. Only after the decision has been made, as to the particular product or level of quality desired, should a librarian ask a vendor to do complete furniture layouts or write elaborate furniture specifications for a project. If a librarian is not genuinely interested in a product, s/he should not waste a salesperson's time. A purchaser is not doing a vendor a favor by "letting" her/him work on a project in order to make all parties involved think the work is being spread around. A vendor cannot be expected to be up front and frank with the purchaser, if the librarian is playing games.

2. It is the responsibility of the librarian to educate and inform all parties who will eventually be involved in awarding a contract. The education process should go on throughout the decision-making process. If a library or friends' board, purchasing agent, or administrator will ultimately have some say in regard to the purchase, it is important to make sure that that person or group agrees with the librarian concerning what product(s) will be acceptable *before* the project is bid. All parties should agree on the level of quality expected and be prepared to back up the librarian when the low bid is not an acceptable item. (It is a great waste of time for everyone involved if all of the standards and stipulations of the bid document are thrown in the trash when the bids come in. In other words, don't specify a top-of-the-line BMW if you're only willing to accept a Yugo when the bids come in.)

3. The librarian should ask for a reasonable amount of information regarding delivery dates without harassing the supplier.

4. If the completed furniture has not been made according to specifications in regard to construction, materials, design, or quality, the librarian is obligated to reject it and demand that the job be done correctly. It is unfair to reputable manufacturers and vendors for a library to accept items that do not fulfill the contract. The practice of accepting inferior goods allows dishonest

companies to stay in business, and lowers the standards of the industry for everyone.

5. Once a project is installed, the librarian has a responsibility to go over all items carefully to make sure that any problems are called to the attention of the supplier immediately. It is better to ask a question or point out a problem and attempt to work out a solution than to let it go and then gripe about the mistake later. In many cases, the problem may be easily corrected. No project is perfect; be prepared to compromise in working out solutions.

6. A vendor cannot be expected to correct a problem that has nothing to do with the manufacture of the product, but rather, is a problem with the situation or environment in which the item is being installed. For example, if wall shelving cannot be properly installed because the wall is crooked, it is not the responsibility of the installer to straighten the wall. Once again, you get what you pay for. If a book shelf made of particleboard, rather than lumber core, is specified and purchased, the vendor cannot be expected to replace a sagging shelf with one of solid wood.

Summary

It would be wonderful if all librarians and all manufacturers and vendors could be depended upon to act responsibly and with integrity in all situations. Unfortunately this is not the case. There are members of every profession who do not act ethically, or in the best interests of others with the same job. For example, salespeople in the library furniture business know that one vendor—the one whose products are specified—has put time into the project already, time for which there may or may not be compensation, depending on how the bid is awarded. Vendors of integrity, who want the process to work for both the buyer and seller, will not put the purchaser in a bind by submitting a low bid for an unapproved alternate that confuses the award process. If the librarian has made a decision based on a thorough investigation of what is available, s/he has a right to choose which furniture is best for the project. Unfortunately, not all salespeople want to accept this, and will low-bid an alternate that meets only *some* of the specifications, on the chance that the buyer will not stand behind his document and will make an award for an item that does not meet specs. In this case, the vendor who worked on the project, and any others who bid to specifications, have been treated unfairly by both the library and the other vendor.

Different librarians like different products, and there are enough projects for vendors who sell a good product to get their share of the market without resorting to unethical behavior. The library that does not stand behind its bid, and gives in to intimidation or threats, does a disservice to other libraries as well as to the salespeople of integrity in the business. The contract also gives the questionable salesperson a better chance of staying in business.

Situations sometimes occur in which a librarian acts responsibly and in good faith to make sure a bid is awarded for a particular product, but, because of some unexpected occurrence, the bid is awarded to a vendor other than the one who put in the work on developing the specifications, did space planning, etc. Sometimes unknown factors arise only after the bids are opened. Both suppliers and customers who understand the furniture market know that there are circumstances that cannot be controlled ahead of time, and that there is always the possibility that the bid will not be awarded as expected.

In summary, the selection of functional, attractive and easy-to-maintain library furnishings begins by determining the needs of the library and collecting information about what products are available. Once products equal to the level of quality desired are chosen, both the vendor and the librarian have responsibilities regarding the bid and purchase process. Sound decisions and responsible actions on both sides of the process will ensure that the library gets the most for its money.

List of Manufacturers

Acme Visible Records
Magic Aisle
1000 Allview Drive
Crozet, Virginia 22932
800-368-2077

Local Dealer:

_____
_____
_____
_____

Adden Furniture
26 Jackson Street
Lowell, Massachusetts 01852
(508) 454-7848

Local Dealer:

_____
_____
_____
_____

Adjustable Steel Products Company
276 Fifth Avenue, Suite 906
New York, New York 10001
(212) 686-1030

Local Dealer:

_____
_____
_____
_____

Advance Manufacturing
A Gaylord Company
P. O. Box 60689
Los Angeles, California 90060-0689
(213) 637-2752

Local Dealer:

_____
_____
_____
_____

Aurora Steel Products
580 South Lake Street
Aurora, Illinois 60507
(312) 892-7696

Local Dealer:

_____
_____
_____
_____

Berco
2210 Montrose Avenue
St. Louis, Missouri 63104
(314) 772-4700

Local Dealer:

_____
_____
_____
_____

Borroughs Division
Lear Siegler, Inc.
3002 North Burdick Street
Kalamazoo, Michigan 49007-1291
800-253-4083

Local Dealer:

_____
_____
_____
_____

Brodart Company
1609 Memorial Avenue
Williamsport, Pennsylvania 17705
800-233-8467

Local Dealer:

_____
_____
_____
_____

Buckstaff Company
1127 South Main Street
Oshkosh, Wisconsin 54901
(414) 235-5890

Local Dealer:

_____
_____
_____
_____

Corry-Hiebert
511 East Carpenter Freeway
Irving, Texas 75062
(214) 506-9500

Local Dealer:

_____
_____
_____
_____

The Danish Library Design Bureau
1412 East North Belt, Suite 120
Houston, Texas 77032
(713) 442-4334

Local Dealer:

_____
_____
_____
_____

Demco
Box 7488
Madison, Wisconsin 53707
800-356-1200

Local Dealer:

_____
_____
_____
_____

Estey Company
Division of Tennsco Corporation
P. O. Box 606
Dickson, Tennessee 37055
800-251-8184

Local Dealer:

_____
_____
_____
_____

Filing Equipment Inc. (FEI)
P. O. Box 457
Ringgold, Georgia 30736
800-241-5246

Local Dealer:

_____
_____
_____
_____

GF Furniture Systems
4944 Belmont Avenue
Youngstown, Ohio 44501
(216) 759-8888

Local Dealer:

_____
_____
_____
_____

Gaylord Brothers
Box 4901
Syracuse, New York 13221-4901
800-634-6307

Local Dealer:

_____
_____
_____
_____

Gressco Limited
2702 International Lane, Suite 108
P. O. Box 7444
Madison, Wisconsin 53707
(608) 244-4999

Local Dealer:

_____
_____
_____

Group Four Furniture
25-5 Connell Court
Toronto, Ontario
Canada M8Z 1E8
(416) 251-1128

Local Dealer:

_____
_____
_____
_____

Haworth
One Haworth Center
Holland, Michigan 49423
(616) 392-5961

Local Dealer:

_____
_____
_____
_____

Highsmith Company
W5527 Highway 106
P. O. Box 800
Fort Atkinson, Wisconsin
   53538-0800
800-558-3899

Local Dealer:

_____
_____
_____
_____

Howe Furniture Company
12 Cambridge Drive
P. O. Box 3086
Trumbull, Connecticut 06611
(203) 374-7833

Local Dealer:

_____
_____
_____
_____

**Interior Woodworking Corporation
   (IWC)**
67742 County Road 23
New Paris, Indiana 46553
(219) 831-4811

Local Dealer:

_____
_____
_____

**International Contract Furnishings
   (ICF)**
305 East 63rd Street
New York, New York 10021
(212) 750-0900

Local Dealer:

_____
_____
_____
_____

International Library Furniture
2140 South Main
Fort Worth, Texas 76110
(817) 926-8682

Local Dealer:

_____
_____
_____
_____

Jasper Chair Company
P. O. Box 311
Jasper, Indiana 47546
(812) 482-5239

Local Dealer:

_____
_____
_____
_____

Johnson Industries
1424 Davis Road
Elgin, Illinois 60123
(312) 695-1242

Local Dealer:

_____
_____
_____
_____

JSI-Jasper Seating
932 Mill Street
P. O. Box 231
Jasper, Indiana 47546
800-622-5661

Local Dealer:

_____
_____
_____

Jysky
1412 East North Belt, Suite 120
Houston, Texas 77032
(713) 442-4334

Local Dealer:

_____
_____
_____
_____

Kardex
P. O. Box 171
Marietta, Ohio 45750
800-848-9761

Local Dealer:

_____
_____
_____
_____

Kinetics Furniture
110 Carrier Drive
Rexdale, Ontario
Canada M9W 5R1
(416) 675-4300

Local Dealer:

_____
_____
_____
_____

Knoll International
655 Madison Avenue
New York, New York 10021
800-223-1354

Local Dealer:

_____
_____
_____
_____

Krueger International
P. O. Box 8100
Green Bay, Wisconsin 54308
(414) 468-8100

Local Dealer:

_____
_____
_____

Lakeland Chair
46320 West 10 Mile Road
Novi, Michigan 48050
800-232-4247

Local Dealer:

_____
_____
_____
_____

Library Bureau
801 Park Avenue
Herkimer, New York 13350
(315) 866-1330

Local Dealer:

_____
_____
_____

Library Steel Stacks
1412 East North Belt, Suite 120
Houston, Texas 77032
(713) 442-4334

Local Dealer:

_____
_____
_____
_____

Lundia Storage Systems
600 Capitol Way
Jacksonville, Illinois 62650
(217) 243-8585

Local Dealer:

_____
_____
_____

MJ Industries
P. O. Box 259
Georgetown, Massachusetts 01833
(508) 352-6190

Local Dealer:

_____
_____
_____

Ron McDole
P. O. Box 2979
Brooke Road
Ft. Collier Industrial Estates
Winchester, Virginia 22601
(703) 667-7983

Local Dealer:

_____
_____
_____

Meridian
P. O. Box 668
18558 171st Avenue
Spring Lake, Michigan 49456
(616) 846-0280

Local Dealer:

_____
_____
_____

Metropolitan Furniture Corporation
245 East Harris Avenue
South San Francisco, California
   94080-6807
(415) 871-6222

Local Dealer:

_____
_____
_____

Herman Miller
8500 Byron Road
Zeeland, Michigan 49464
800-851-1196

Local Dealer:

_____
_____
_____

Modulex
2920 Wolff Street
Racine, Wisconsin 53404
800-632-4321

Local Dealer:

_____
_____
_____

Mohawk Midland Manufacturing
P. O. Box 226
7733 Gross Point Road
Skokie, Illinois 60076-0226
(312) 677-0333

Local Dealer:

_____

_____

_____

Montel
Aetnastack Division
35 East Elizabeth Avenue, Suite 1B
Bethlehem, Pennsylvania 18018
(215) 691-8525

Local Dealer:

_____

_____

_____

Thomas Moser
Cobbs Bridge Road
New Gloucester, Maine 04260
(207) 926-4446

Local Dealer:

_____

_____

_____

Nemschoff Chairs
2218 West Water Street
Sheboygan, Wisconsin 53081
(414) 457-7726

Local Dealer:

_____

_____

_____

Redco
P. O. Box 1608
1601 Madison, Southeast
Grand Rapids, Michigan 49501
800-253-8106

Local Dealer:

_____

_____

_____

Rudd International
1025 Thomas Jefferson Street,
Northwest
Washington, D. C. 20007
(202) 333-5600

Local Dealer:

_____

_____

_____

Russ Bassett
P. O. Box 249
8189 Byron Road
Whittier, California 90608
800-624-4728

Local Dealer:

_____

_____

_____

Spacemaster Systems
Reflector Hardware Corporation
1400 North 25th Avenue
Melrose Park, Illinois 60160
(312) 345-2500

Local Dealer:

_____

_____

_____

Spacesaver Corporation
1450 Janesville Avenue
Ft. Atkinson, Wisconsin 53538
(414) 563-6362

Local Dealer:

_____

_____

_____

Steelcase/Stow and Davis
901 44th Street Southeast
Grand Rapids, Michigan 49501
800-227-2960

Local Dealer:

_____

_____

_____

Storwal International
P. O. Box 250
1000 Olympic Drive
Pembroke, Ontario
Canada K8A 6X5
800-267-0747

Local Dealer:

_____

_____

_____

Sunar Hauserman
5711 Grant Avenue
Cleveland, Ohio 44105
(216) 883-1400

Local Dealer:

_____

_____

_____

Supreme Equipment and Systems
170 53rd Street
Brooklyn, New York 11232
(718) 439-3800

Local Dealer:

_____

_____

_____

TAB Products
1400 Page Mill Road
Palo Alto, California 94304
800-672-3109

Local Dealer:

_____

_____

_____

Texwood
P. O. Box 6280
3508 East 1st Street
Austin, Texas 78762
(512) 385-3323

Local Dealer:

_____

_____

_____

Tuohy Furniture Corporation
42 St. Albans Place
Chatfield, Minnesota 55923
800-533-1696

Local Dealer:

_____
_____
_____
_____

Vecta Contract
1800 South Great Southwest
   Parkway
Grand Prairie, Texas 75050
(214) 641-2860

Local Dealer:

_____
_____
_____
_____

Westinghouse Electric Corporation
4300 36th Street
Grand Rapids, Michigan 49508
800-445-5045

Local Dealer:

_____
_____
_____
_____

White Office Systems
50 Boright Avenue
Kenilworth, New Jersey 07033
(201) 272-8888

Local Dealer:

_____
_____
_____
_____

The Worden Company
P. O. Box 1227
199 East 17th Street
Holland, Michigan 49422
800-678-0199

Local Dealer:

_____
_____
_____

Other addresses:

Architectural Woodwork Institute
2310 S. Walter Reed Drive
Arlington, Virginia 22206
(703) 671-9100

Underwriters Laboratories
333 Pfingsten Road
Northbrook, Illinois 60062
(312) 272-8800

Bibliography

Architectural Woodwork Institute. *Architectural Woodwork Quality Standards, Guide Specifications and Quality Certification Program*. 4th ed. Arlington, Virginia: Architectural Woodwork Institute, 1985.

Boardman, Robert. 1981. "Particle Board vs. Lumber Core, Panel Materials Used in Furniture and Cabinet Construction." The Worden Company, Holland, Michigan. Photocopy.

Buyers Laboratory, Inc. "Lateral Roll-Out File Cabinets." *Library Technology Reports* 18, no. 4 (July-August 1982): 423–473.

Cohen, Aaron, and Elaine Cohen. *Designing and Space Planning for Libraries: A Behavioral Guide*. New York: R. R. Bowker, 1979.

Deasy, C. M., and Thomas E. Lasswell. *Designing Places for People: A Handbook on Human Behavior for Architects, Designers, and Facility Managers*. New York: Whitney Library of Design, Watson-Guptill, 1985.

Eckelman, Carl A. "Evaluating the Strength of Library Chairs and Tables." *Library Technology Reports* 13, no. 4 (July 1977): 341–433.

———. "The Use of Performance Tests and Quality-Assurance Programs in the Selection of Library Chairs." *Library Technology Reports* 18, no. 5 (September-October 1982): 483–571.

Ehrlich, Jeffrey, and Marc Mannheimer. *The Carpenter's Manifesto*. New York: Holt, Rinehart and Winston, 1977.

Feirer, John L. *Cabinetmaking and Millwork*. 2d. ed. Peoria, Illinois: Scribner, 1983.

Hanna, Herbert L., and Nancy H. Knight. "Movable Compact Shelving: A Survey of U.S. Suppliers and Library Users." *Library Technology Reports* 17, no. 1 (January-February 1981): 7–105.

Hoadley, R. Bruce. *Understanding Wood: A Craftsman's Guide to Wood Technology*. Newtown, CT: Taunton Press, 1980.

Lushington, Nolan, and Willis N. Mills, Jr. *Libraries Designed for Users: A Planning Handbook*. Hamden, Connecticut: Library Professional Publications, Shoe String Press, 1980.

Macdonald, Hugh. "Designing a Reference Desk." *Texas Library Journal* 62 (Fall 1986): 175–178.

Mallery, Mary S., and Ralph E. DeVore. *A Sign System For Libraries*. Chicago: American Library Association, 1982.

Metcalf, Keyes. *Planning Academic and Research Library Buildings*. 2d ed. by Philip D. Leighton and David C. Weber. Chicago: American Library Association, 1986.

Pollet, Dorothy, and Peter C. Haskell, eds. *Sign Systems for Libraries: Solving the Wayfinding Problem*. New York: R. R. Bowker, 1979.

Poole, Frazer G., and Alphonse F. Trezza, eds. *The Procurement of Library Furnishings, Specifications, Bid Documents, and Evaluation*. Proceedings of the Library Equipment Institute conducted at New York, New York, July 7–9, 1966, sponsored by the Library Administration Division. Chicago: American Library Association, 1969.

Pulgram, William, and Richard E. Stonis. *Designing the Automated Office, a Guide for Architects, Interior Designers, Space Planners, and Facility Managers*. New York: Whitney Library of Design, Watson-Guptill Publications, 1984.

Reynolds, Linda, and Stephen Barrett. *Signs and Guiding for Libraries*. London: Clive Bingley Limited, 1981.

Reznikoff, S. C. *Interior Graphic and Design Standards*. New York: Whitney Library of Design, Watson-Guptill Publications, 1986.

———. *Specifications for Commercial Interiors, Professional Liabilities, Regulations, and Performance Criteria*. New York: Whitney Library of Design, Watson-Guptill Publications, 1979.

Smith, Charles R. "Compact-Shelving Specifications." *Library Administration and Management* 1, no. 3 (June 1987): 94–95.

Steelcase, Inc. *The Office Environment Index, 1987 Summary Report*. Conducted by Louis Harris and Associates. Grand Rapids, Michigan: Steelcase, 1987.

Index

CAROL R. BROWN

Ms. Brown is the owner of a consulting firm, Carol Brown Associates, which specializes in the planning of library buildings and the design of library and office interiors. She previously held the position of Assistant Chief of Branch Services at Houston Public Library, after joining the library as Adult Specialist in the Office of Material Selection and advancing to become Manager of Jungman Branch. Having formerly worked as reference librarian and Assistant Undergraduate Librarian at Indiana University, she has a wide range of library experience. Ms. Brown holds an M.A. in Library Science from Indiana University and a B.A. in Fine Arts and English from Cornell College. She has consulted in collection development, communications, the planning of library buildings, and furniture design for many years.